NATIONAL INDEX OF P

A Guide to Anglican, Roman Catholic
and Non-Conformist Registers
together with information on Bishop's Transcripts,
modern copies and Marriage licences.

VOLUME 9

PART 5

LONDON & MIDDLESEX

Second edition (Revised)

Compiled by
Cliff Webb, M.A., F.S.G.

General Editor
Cliff Webb, M.A., F.S.G.

SOCIETY OF GENEALOGISTS ENTERPRISES LTD

Published by
Society of Genealogists Enterprises Limited
14 Charterhouse Buildings
Goswell Road
London EC1M 7BA

© 2002 Society of Genealogists Enterprises Limited

ISBN 1 903462 69 X

British Library Cataloguing in Publication Data
A CIP Catalogue record for this book is available from the British Library

Volumes of the *National Index of Parish Registers* already published

Volume 1   **General Sources of Births, Marriages and Deaths before 1837.**
            Parish Registers, Marriage Licenses, Monumental Inscriptions, Newspapers,
            Clandestine Marriages, Divorce, Mediaeval Sources, Other Records. General
            Bibliography.

Volume 2   **Sources for Nonconformist Genealogy and Family History.**
            The Three Denominations (Presbyterians, Independents and Baptists), Society of
            Friends, Moravians, Methodists, Foreign Churches, Other Denominations.

Volume 3   **Sources for Roman Catholic Genealogy and Family History.**
            With a short section on Jewish Records., contributed by Edgar Samuel. Index
            to Volumes 1, 2 and 3.

Volume 4   **South East England.**
            Kent, Surrey and Sussex (a revised edition of Surrey has appeared as Volume 4
            Part 1 of the series).

Volume 5   **South Midlands and Welsh Border.**
            Gloucestershire, Herefordshire, Oxfordshire, Shropshire, Warwickshire and
            Worcestershire (a revised edition of Shropshire has appeared as Volume 5 Part 1
            of the series).

Volume 6   **North and East Midlands.**
            Part 1: Staffordshire. Part 2: Nottinghamshire.
            Part 3: Leicestershire and Rutland. Part 4: Lincolnshire. Part 5: Derbyshire.

Volume 7   **East Anglia.**
            Part 1: Suffolk. Part 2: Cambridgeshire. Part 3: Norfolk.

Volume 8   **The West of England.**
            Part 1: Berkshire. Part 2: Wiltshire. Part 3: Somerset.
            Part 4: Cornwall. Part 5: Devon. Part 6: Hampshire. Part 7: Dorset

Volume 9   **Home Counties (North of the Thames) and South East Midlands.**
            Part 1: Bedfordshire, Huntingdonshire. Part 2: Northamptonshire.
            Part 3: Buckinghamshire. Part 4: Essex. Part 5: London and Middlesex.
            Part 6: Hertfordshire.

Volume 10   **North West England.**
            Part 1: Cheshire. Part 2: Lancashire. Part 3: Cumberland and Westmorland.

Volume 11   **North East England.**
            Part 1: Durham and Northumberland.
            Part 2: Yorkshire (North and East Ridings and York). Part 3: Yorkshire (West).

Volume 12   **Sources for Scottish Genealogy and Family History.**
            Historical background. Parish Registers, Ancillary Sources. Nonconformists,
            Bibliography.

Volume 13   **Parish Registers of Wales.**

Volume 14   **Nonconformist Registers of Wales.**

Volume 15   **British Islands.**
            Part 1: Channel Islands and the Isle of Man.

Society of Genealogists Enterprises Limited is a wholly owned subsidiary of Society of Genealogists,
a registered charity, no. 233701. Company Number 3899591 VAT Number 749 5602103

CITY OF LONDON

Introductory note   5
City of London   5
Record offices and libraries   5
Ecclesiastical divisions and original parish registers   5
Bishop's transcripts   7
Modern copies of parish registers
Printed   7
Typescript and manuscript   7
Microform   8
Marriage indexes   8
Allegations for marriage licences   8
Cemeteries   8
Nonconformist records   8
Livery Companies   8
Appendix: printed registers of London and Middlesex   9
Abbreviations   12
Parish listing   13

INTRODUCTORY NOTE

Recent volumes of the National Index of Parish Registers have listed registers of all churches and chapels in the county in question, regardless of the original cut-off date of 1837. Much work was done by Mrs Doreen Willcocks to collect this information for London and Middlesex. However, with the growth of population of London, it became apparent that such a volume would be very large indeed, and would have to be on sale at a prohibitive price. It was decided, therefore, that in the case of London and Middlesex, the parish registers, etc. would only be listed for churches and chapels founded in 1837 or before.

It was also decided that it was necessary to treat the City of London and the County of Middlesex in two separate sequences, and provide two separate introductions to them.

CITY OF LONDON

The City of London is the 'square mile' (actually rather broader than it is deep) which was enclosed by the Roman and early medieval walls. London is a twin city, the City of London having always been the commercial heart of the country, and the City of Westminster a mile or so to the west being the administrative and political centre. They did not form a continuous built-up area until the eighteenth century. As the Metropolitan area expanded, so more and more of the population lived outside the City of London, but until the mid-eighteenth century the vast majority of people lived in this small area. As that century continued however, more and more of the City was taken over by warehouses, shops and offices, and the population started to fall, at first slowly, and then steeply, until by the beginning of this century only about five thousand people actually lived in the City, mainly caretakers and their families.

The City has always enjoyed a separate administration from the rest of London and Middlesex. The City is run by the Corporation of London and by a Common Council, it was never under the juridiction of the Greater London Council. Its archives, and those of the churches within it, likewise, have not been deposited with the London Metropolitan Archives. Indeed with the demise of the Greater London Council, the London Metropolitan Archives was placed under the overall jurisdiction of the Corporation of London, though this does not effect the location of records.

The overwhelming majority of City parish records have been deposited at the Guildhall Library. There also, most of the ancient Livery Company records are also deposited. Until the early nineteenth century to practise a trade in the City you needed to be a member of a Livery Company, and their records are an invaluable supplement to parish records.

A few parishes, such as St Botolph Aldgate, are partially within and partially without the City area. In records this is sometimes shown in the forms St Botolph Aldgate, Middlesex and St Botolph Aldgate, London, sometimes as St Botolph Aldgate Within and St Botolph Aldgate Without. Such parishes have generally been listed in both sections of this book, though one or two marginal cases, such as Whitechapel, which had only six houses in the City area are merely noted in one section.

RECORD OFFICES AND LIBRARIES

Guildhall Library, Aldermanbury, London EC2P 2EJ. 9.30 am to 4.45 pm Monday to Saturday
(Tel: 0207-260-1683)
This holds virtually all City parish registers, plus the Middlesex registers of St Andrew Holborn and St Katharine by the Tower, and a wealth of other records of City parishes.

For other record offices see Middlesex section.

ECCLESIASTICAL DIVISIONS AND ORIGINAL PARISH REGISTERS

The City of London is and has always been entirely in the diocese of London, apart from the Peculiars. All Hallows Bread Street, All Hallows Lombard Street, St Dionis Backchurch, St Dunstan in the East, St John the Evangelist, St Leonard Eastcheap, St Mary Aldermary, St Mary Bothaw, St Mary le Bow, St Michael Crooked Lane, St Michael Paternoster Royal, St Pancras Soper

Lane and St Vedast formed the Peculiar of the Deanery of the Arches. St Giles Cripplegate, St Gregory by St Paul's and St Helen were in the Peculiar of the Dean and Chapter of St Paul's. St Peter ad Vincula in the Tower was a Chapel Royal, the Tower itself being extra-parochial.

Various other areas, mainly on the edge of the City were extra-parohial, chiefly the sites of monasteries and the Inns of Court. Some such as Bridewell, had chapels, others were served by nearby churches.

Perhaps because of its status as the nation's capital and its continuous prosperity, and despite considerable destruction during World War II, the City has many early registers, indeed its average starting date (1578) is by far the earliest for any English county. A large number of registers were lost in World War II, but fortunately, printed editions had been published of the vast majority of the early registers which were destroyed by enemy action. In the compilation which follows, printed registers are counted, even if the originals have been lost.

In the Great Fire of London in 1666 no less than 87 (of 108) parish churches as well as St Paul's Cathedral were destroyed. Many were not rebuilt, and it is surprising that not only would it seem that few registers were lost in the Great Fire, but that pre-Fire registers survive for the majority even of those churches which were not rebuilt. However, no early registers survive for St Benet Sherehog, St Leonard Foster Lane and St Margaret New Fish Street.

Two City parishes have registers starting before 1538; St James Garlickhythe, which starts in 1535, and St Mary Bothaw which starts in 1536. 23 start in 1538 (All Hallows Bread Street, All Hallows Honey Lane, Christ Church Greyfriars (in the form of its predecessor church St Nicholas Shambles), St Andrew Hubbard, St Benet Fink, St Dionis Backchurch, St Laurence Pountney, St Lawrence Jewry, St Leonard Eastcheap, St Martin Ludgate, St Mary the Virgin Aldermanbury, St Mary le Bow, St Mary Woolnoth, St Matthew Friday Street, St Michael Bassishaw, St Michael Crooked Lane, St Mildred Poultry, St Nicholas Cole Abbey, St Olave Old Jewry, St Pancras Soper Lane, St Peter Cornhill, St Peter Westcheap and St Stephen Coleman Street). Five more start in 1539 (St Antholin, St Clement Eastcheap, St Martin Pomeroy, St Mary Magdalen Old Fish Street and St Nicholas Acons). Thus well over a quarter of all City churches have records going back to within a year or two of the beginning of parish registers.

Seven more parishes have registers beginning before 1558, and no less than 24 begin in that year and six in the year after. Thus 67 parishes or over 60% have registers beginning within a year of the beginning of the reign of Queen Elizabeth I. Ten more parishes have registers starting before 1600 and eleven more start before 1650. Sixteen parishes have registers beginning in the 1650-1700 period, and just one (St Nicholas Olave, starting in 1704) has no pre-1700 registers surviving.

The Guildhall Library have been successful in securing the deposit of the registers of all the City parish churches other than All Hallows Barking (where it is believed arrangements are being made to allow the Genealogical Society of Utah to film the registers) and St Bartholomew the Less (among the archives of the Hospital, a full transcript is available on microfiche). The Royal Chapel of St Peter ad Vincula has also not deposited and for this there is no full copy available.

Also in public custody are the Fleet Registers. These are the records kept of various more or less clandestine marriages 'under the rules of the Fleet' until 1754, when new legislation put paid to such practices. The several hundred registers and notebooks are an important source for the 1700-1754 period for the whole country, especially the south-east, and are deposited as Public Record Office class RG 7. Mark Herber has transcribed, index and published three volumes of transcripts from these registers, but the majority remain uncopied and unindexed.

At the Public Record Office also are two other sources of national importance. Bunhill Fields was the chief burial place for Nonconformists from the Metropolitan area, but people were brought from all over the country to be buried there. An index to these burials is now available on microfiche. Dr Williams Library from 1742 maintained a register of births, largely but not exclusively of Nonconformists, which again was used by people from the whole country. A similar registry was established by the Methodists in the 1820s. Entries from both of these are included in the CD Rom *Vital Records Index - British Isles*.

BISHOP'S TRANSCRIPTS

The bishop's transcripts of the City of London are very sparse. There are no transcripts before 1629. For the period 1629-31 there survive transcripts for 35 parishes (including some from churches destroyed in the Great Fire for which no registers survive at all). From the period 1639-1640 they survive for 39 parishes. Nineteen parishes have returns in the 1665-1666 period. Ten parishes in the Deanery of the Arches have transcripts starting in 1799.

The main sequence of transcripts only starts in 1800 for the majority of parishes. 23 parishes have *no* earlier transcript at all, six sequences start in 1801, and four in 1802. One starts in 1809, and in 1813 four more start (St Faith, St Giles Cripplegate, St Gregory and St Helen), St Paul's Cathedral begins in 1814, and St Pancras Soper Lane does not start until 1817. Noticeably, three of these last parishes as well as St Paul's itself were peculiars of the Dean and Chapter.

London transcripts do not extend to a late period. Many end in the 1830s, and few postdate the 1850s.

Now doubt this paucity may be explained, at least in part, by their total neglect by those responsible for their care. In the *Athenaeum* of 5 July 1890 (7th Ser. 11 p.94) "W.C.W." refers to the Bishop of London's transcripts which were stored at that time in St Paul's Cathedral: 'I was once taken to see those transcripts in the dome - some cartloads of them, in a pile, covered with a pall of black dust'. It would seem likely that at some point somebody ordered the destruction of the pre-1800 transcripts; it seems unlikely that they were never made except perhaps for the Peculiar of the Dean and Chapter.

MODERN COPIES OF PARISH REGISTERS

PRINTED

The City of London has been fortunate in that antiquarians have always taken a great interest in it, and many transcripts have been printed of its parish registers. Indeed the register section of the Harleian Society published mainly City registers, and it is due to this series, as noted above, that relatively few of the registers lost by enemy action in World War II did not have their informational content saved. A list of printed London and Middlesex registers including the Harleian Series constitutes an Appendix to this introduction.

It is now generally regarded as uneconomic to print registers, and most recent work in the field has been produced on microfiche.

TYPESCRIPT AND MANUSCRIPT

Both the Society of Genealogists and the Guildhall Library have extensive collections of unprinted transcripts which partially duplicate each other. There are two major collections at the Guildhall Library, the first compiled by W.H. Challen is almost entirely of marriages, the second by myself, has concentrated on finishing registers which had been partially printed by the Harleian Society, and on completing marriage registers missing from other collections. The Society of Genealogists has a burial index to the City, compiled by Percival Boyd, but extracting only male adults (this source should be available shortly on the Origins website - see page 8). I compiled a burial index for the period 1813-1853 for most of the smaller, inner parishes of the City. Monnica Stevens has in a series of works completed that index for the City and is working on surrounding cemeteries and churches. All these latter have been published on microfiche.

In addition to these, both libraries contain a large number of transcripts made by various people over the years. There is also a collection of material at the College of Arms, collected by several late nineteenth-century antiquaries, notably Colonel Chester. These contain material no longer extant or difficult of access (e.g. St Peter Westcheap and the Savoy Chapel), and it is highly desirable that further copies be made of them.

ORIGINS

This pay to view website is linked with the Society of Genealogists. Members of the Society have a certain number of free remote searches as part of their annual subscription, and also enjoy unlimited free access in the Society's own library.

The website has much material of interest to London researchers, including Boyd's Marriage Index, London Marriage Allegations and the published apprenticeship registers. Any list of its contents is out of date before it can be published and researchers should consult the website itself for details.

MICROFORM

All the early registers deposited at the Guildhall Library have been filmed, and in the vast majority of cases even the latest ones have been to save wear and tear on the originals. Copies of most of these films are at Salt Lake City and are thus available at Family History Centres throughout the world for a small handling charge. The Genealogical Society of Utah have also, of course, filmed all the Nonconformist registers at the Public Record Office. Because of the comprehensiveness of this coverage space has not been wasted listing films.

This comprehensiveness is reflected, naturally enough, in the coverage of the International Genealogical Index, though relatively few London marriages yet appear in the Index.

MARRIAGE INDEXES

Boyd's Index covers part or all the pre-1837 marriages for ninety City parishes. Boyd's Index is available at the Society of Genealogists and on microform at Family History Centres. The Guildhall Library has a copy of the London and Middlesex section. The index is also availabe on the Origins website (see above).

The Pallot Index is housed at the Institute of Heraldic and Genealogical Studies, 80-82 Northgate, Canterbury, Kent CT1 1BA. This index covers mainly the 1780-1837 period, and from 1800 is virtually complete for the City of London. The index has been digitised, and is available on CD Rom. Purchasers of the CD Rom may link back to look, through the internet, at the original slips.

ALLEGATIONS FOR MARRIAGE LICENCES

Various authorities could issue marriage licences to residents of the City of London and Middlesex. They, their records and lists and indexes to them are listed in the introduction to the Middlesex section. Indexes to most of them prior to 1837 are available on the Origins website.

CEMETERIES

A list of all the Cemeteries in the Metropolitan area, and the location of their records is readily available in *Greater London Cemeteries and Crematoria* (comp. P.S. Wolfston, revised C.R. Webb, Society of Genealogists, 1999), and this information is not therefore repeated here.

NONCONFORMIST RECORDS

Details of various Nonconformist denominations will be found in the introduction to the Middlesex section of this book.

LIVERY COMPANIES

Most City Livery Companies have deposited records at the Guildhall Library. The Clothworkers, Drapers, Goldsmiths, Leathesellers, Mercers, Salters and Stationers retain their own. In some records, especially early ones, there are direct references to vital events, e.g. when a member died, it was sometimes minuted. Much more often there are indirect references in the great series of apprenticeship registers, which also are one of the best sources for the origins of Londoners before 1800. A series of editions of these has been published by the Society of Genealogists.

APPENDIX: PRINTED REGISTERS OF LONDON AND MIDDLESEX

For convenience all printed London and Middlesex registers will be found in this one list, except for the pubications of the Huguenot Society, which will be found listed in *London and Middlesex: A Genealogical Bibliography*, Stuart A. Raymond (1994).

A. Harleian Society Register Section, London and Middlesex registers only:

1	St Peter Cornhill CMB 1538-1666, ed. W.G. Leveson Gower (1877)
3	St Dionis Backchurch CMB 1538-1754, ed. Joseph L. Chester (1878)
4	St Peter Cornhill CB 1667-1774, M 1673-1754, ed. W.G. Leveson Gower (1879)
5	St Mary Aldermary CMB 1553-1754, ed. Joseph L. Chester (1880)
6	St Thomas Apostle CMB 1558-1754, ed. Joseph L. Chester (1881)
7	St Michael Cornhill 1546-1754, ed. Joseph L. Chester (1882)
8	St Antholin, Budge Row, London CMB 1538-1754; St.John the Baptist on Wallbrook CMB 1682-1754, ed. Joseph L. Chester and George J. Armytage (1883)
9	St James Clerkenwell C 1551-1700, ed. Robert Hovenden (1884)
10	St James Clerkenwell C 1701-1754, ed. Robert Hovenden (1885)
11	St George Hanover Square M 1725-1787, ed. John H. Chapman (1886)
13	St James Clerkenwell M 1551-1754, ed. Robert Hovenden (1887)
14	St George Hanover Square M 1788-1809, ed. John H. Chapman (1888)
15	St George's Chapel, Mayfair, ed. George J. Armytage (1889)
16	Kensington CMB 1539-1675, ed. F.N. Macnamara and A. Story-Maskelyne (1890)
17	St James Clerkenwell B 1551-1665, ed. Robert Hovenden (1891)
18	Charterhouse chapel, C 1696-1836, M 1671-1754, 1837-90, B 1695-1854 ed. Francis Collins (1892)
19	St James Clerkenwell B 1666-1719, ed. Robert Hovenden (1893)
20	St James Clerkenwell B 1720-1754, ed. Robert Hovenden (1894)
21	Christ Church, Newgate 1538-1754, ed. Willoughby A. Littledale (1895)
22	St George Hanover Square M 1810-1823, ed. George J. Armytage (1896)
24	St George Hanover Square M 1824-1837, ed. George J. Armytage (1897)
25	St Martin in the Fields 1550-1619, ed. Thomas Mason (1898)
26	St Paul's Cathedral, ed. John W. Clay (1899)
29-30	St Vedast Foster Lane and St Michael le Querne, ed. Willoughby A. Littledale (1902-1903)
31	St Helen Bishopsgate, ed. W. Bruce Bannerman (1904)
32	St Martin Outwich, ed. W. Bruce Bannerman (1905)
33	St Paul Covent Garden C 1653-1752, ed. William H. Hunt (1906)
34	St Paul Covent Garden C 1752-1837, ed. William H. Hunt (1906)
35	St Paul Covent Garden M 1653-1837, ed. William H. Hunt (1906)
36	St Paul Covent Garden B 1653-1752, ed. William H. Hunt (1908)
37	St Paul Covent Garden B 1752-1853, ed. William H. Hunt (1909)
38-41	St Benet and St Peter, Paul's Wharf, ed. Willoughby A. Littledale (1909-1912)
42	St Mildred Bread St. and St Margaret Moses, ed. W. Bruce Bannerman (1912)
43	All Hallows, Bread St. and St John the Evangelist, Friday St., ed. W.Bruce Bannerman (1913)
44-45	St Mary le Bow, All Hallows Honey Lane and St Pancras Soper Lane, ed. W. Bruce Bannerman (1914-1915)
46	St Olave Hart St. 1563-1700, ed. W. Bruce Bannerman (1916)
47	St Mary le Bone M 1668-1754 and Oxford Chapel M 1736-1754, ed. W. Bruce Bannerman (1917)
48	St Mary le Bone M 1754-1775, ed. W. Bruce Bannerman and R. Bruce Bannerman (1918)
49-50	St Stephen Walbrook and St Benet Sherehog, ed. W. Bruce Bannerman (1919-1920)
51	St Mary le Bone M 1775-1783, ed. W. Bruce Bannerman (1921)
52	St Mary le Bone M 1783-1792, ed. W. Bruce Bannerman (1922)
53	St Mary le Bone M 1792-1796, ed. W. Bruce Bannerman (1923)
54	St Mary le Bone M 1796-1801, ed. W. Bruce Bannerman (1924)
55	St Mary le Bone M 1801-1806, ed. W. Bruce Bannerman (1925)
56	St Mary le Bone M 1806-1809, ed. W. Bruce Bannerman (1926)
57	St Mary le Bone M 1809-1812, ed. W. Bruce Bannerman (1927)
58	St Mary Mounthaw, ed. W. Bruce Bannerman (1928)
59-60	St Mary Somerset, ed. W. Bruce Bannerman (1929-1930)

61-62 St Mary the Virgin, Aldermanbury 1538-1722, ed. W. Bruce Bannerman (1931-1932)
63 St Matthew Friday St. CMB 1538-1812 and St Peter Westcheap M 1754-1812, ed. W. Bruce Bannerman (1933)
64 St Margaret Westminster C 1660-1675, M 1664-1675, B 1660-1662, ed. Lawrence F. Tanner (1935) ·
65 St Mary the Virgin, Aldermanbury 1722-1837, ed. W. Bruce Bannerman (1935)
66 St Martin in the Fields 1619-1636, ed. J.V. Kitto (1936)
67-68 St Clement Eastcheap and St Martin Orgar, ed. A.W. Hughes Clarke (1937-1938)
69 St Dunstan in the East CMB 1558-1654, ed. A.W. Hughes Clarke (1939)
70-71 St Lawrence Jewry and St Mary Magdalen Milk St. CMB 1538-1812, ed. A.W. Hughes Clarke (1940-1941)
72 St Mary Magdalen, Milk St. CMB 1558-1666 and St Michael Bassishaw CMB 1538-1625, ed. A.W. Hughes Clarke (1942)
73-74 St Michael Bassishaw 1626-1892, ed. A.W. Hughes Clarke (1943-1944)
75 St Katherine by the Tower 1584-1625, ed. A.W. Hughes Clarke (1945)
76 St Katherine by the Tower 1626-1665, ed. A.W. Hughes Clarke (1946)
77 St Katherine by the Tower M 1666-1686, ed. A.W. Hughes Clarke (1947)
78-79 St Katherine by the Tower M 1686-1726, ed. R.H. D'Elboux (1949)
80-81 St Katherine by the Tower C 1666-1695, B 1666-1695, ed. R.H. D'Elboux (1952)
84-85 St Dunstan in the East CMB 1653-1691, ed. R.H. D'Elboux (1955)
86-87 St Dunstan in the East C 1692-1758, M 1692-1754, B 1692-1766, ed. R.H. D'Elboux and Winifride Ward (1958)
88 St Margaret Westminster C 1676-1681, M 1676-1682, B 1664-1666, ed. Winifride Ward (1958)
89 St Margaret Westminster C 1681-1688, M 1681-1699, B 1666-1673, ed. Winifride Ward (1977)

New Series 1 Temple Church C 1629-1853, M 1628-1760, ed. G.D. Squibb (1979)

B. Phillimore London and Middlesex Marriages:

a. London ed. W.P.W. Phillimore and G.E. Cokayne

1-4 St James Duke's Place 1664-1668, 1679-1837 (1900-1902)

b. **Middlesex** (vols. 1-8 ed. W.P.W. Phillimore and Thomas Gurney, vol. 9 ed. William McB. and Frank Marcham)

1 Acton 1566-1812; Heston 1559-1812; Hanwell 1570-1812; Harlington 1540-1812; Greenford 1539-1812 (1909)
2 Hillingdon 1559-1812; Hayes 1557-1812; Northolt 1575-1812; Ickenham 1558-1812; Cowley 1563-1812; West Drayton 1568-1812 (1910)
3 Hampton 1657-1812; Twickenham 1538-1812; Teddington 1560-1837 (1911)
4 New Brentford 1618-1812; Hounslow 1708-1812; Stanwell 1632-1812; Sunbury 1566-1812; Ashford 1696-1812; Feltham 1634-1812; Hanworth 1732-1837; Pinner 1654-1837 (1912)
5 Uxbridge 1538-1694; Harefield 1546-1837; Great Stanmore 1599-1837; Enfield 1550-1837 (1914)
6 Edmonton 1557-1837 (1914)
7 Finchley 1560-1837; South Mimms 1558-1837; Monken Hadley 1619-1837 (1915)
8 Ealing 1582-1837 (1927)
9 Tottenham 1558-1837 (1938)

C. Miscellaneous in order of publication:

Somerset House Chapel 1714-1776, ed. James Coleman (1862)
All Hallows London Wall CMB 1559 to 1675, ed. E.B. Jupp and R. Hovenden (1878)
St Christopher le Stocks CMB 1558-1780, ed. Edwin Freshfield, 2 vols. (1882)
Austin Friars 1571-1874, ed. William J.C. Moens (1884)
St Mary Woolnoth and St Mary Woolchurch Haw CMB 1538-1760, ed. J.M.S. Brooke and
     A.W.C. Hallen (1886)
Staines 1644-1694, ed. F.A. Crisp (1886)
St Mary le Strand M 1606-1625, ed. John V.L. Pruyn, *Genealogist* N.S. 4-5 (1887-1888)
St Botolph Bishopsgate C 1558-1690, M 1558-1753, B 1558-1752, ed. A.W.C. Hallen, 3 vols.,
     (1889)
St Nicholas Acons CMB 1539-1812, ed. William Brigg (1890)
Duke Street Chapel, Westminster M 1745-1753 *Miscellanea Genealogica et Heraldica*
     2nd series 3 p.396 (1890)
St Edmund the King and Martyr 1670-1812, ed. William Brigg (1892)
St Mary le Strand M 1653-1660 *Genealogist*, N.S. 10 (1894)
Lincolns Inn Chapel C 1716-1806, M 1695-1754, B 1695-1852 *The records of the Honourable
     Society of Lincoln's Inn* 2 (1896)
Stepney M 1568-1719, ed. Sir T. Colyer-Ferguson (1898-1901)
Harrow 1558-1653, ed. W.O. Hewlett (1899)
St Dunstan in the East M 1606-1625, ed. J.V.L. Pruyn, *Genealogist*, N.S. 11 (1895)
Temple Church B 1628-1853, ed. H.F. Wood (1905)
Isleworth Catholic Registers, ed. Joseph S. Hansom, Catholic Record Society 13 (1913)
St Margaret Westminster 1539-1660, ed. Arthur M. Burke (1914)
St Ethelburga the Virgin C 1671-1914, M 1679-1915, B 1672-1849, ed. W.F. Cobb (1915)
Lincoln's Inn Fields Catholic Registers, ed. C.R. Lindsay, Catholic Record Society 19 (1917)
St George the Martyr, Queen Square C 1710-1740, M 1706-1772 Parish Register Society
     Extra Vol. 1 (1922)
Holy Trinity Knightsbridge 1658-1681, ed. James H. Bloom (1925)
Hammersmith Catholic Registers 1710-1838, ed. Johanna H. Harting, Catholic Record Society
     26-27 (1926-1927)
Registers of the Catholic Chapels Royal and of the Portuguese Embassy Chapel 1662-1829 (M only),
     ed. J.C.M. Weale, Catholic Record Society 38 (1941)
Spanish and Portuguese Jews M 1690-1837, ed. L.D. Barnett and G.H. Whitehill,
     Bevis Marks Records 2 (1949)
Harlington M 1540-1812, ed. Herbert Wilson in *800 years of Harlington parish church* (1926)
Chelsea M 1704-1760, ed. J.S.W. Gibson (1958)
Spanish and Portuguese Jews B 1657-1753, ed. R.D. Barnett, Jewish Historical Society of England
     Miscellanies 6 (1962)
Kensington M 1676-1775, ed. B.R. Curle (1969)
Spanish and Portuguese Jews M 1837-1901, ed. L.D. Barnett and G.H. Whitehill,
     Bevis Marks Records 3 (1973)
St Martin in the Fields, Camden Town Burial Ground B 1806-1856, ed. Jean Alexander, North
     Middlesex FHS, microfiche (1985)
Stepney M 1568-1719, ed. Sir T. Colyer-Ferguson, reprinted on microfiche as their Record
     Publications 143 by Kent FHS (1985)
Holy Trinity Holborn B 1839-1856, ed. V. Payne, North Middlesex FHS, microfiche (1986)
Wembley St John the Evangelist M 1848-1915, ed. D.E. Jones, Central Middlesex FHS, microfiche
     (1986)
Highgate B 1633-1903 North Middlesex FHS, microfiche (1987)
Holy Trinity in the Minories M 1676-1692 East of London FHS, microfiche (1988-1992)
City Road Chapel Burial Ground B 1779-1882 North Middlesex FHS, microfiche (1990)
Poplar B 1824-1838 East of London FHS, microfiche (1991)
Christ Church Spitalfields Banns 1833-1861 East of London FHS, microfiche (1991)
Millbank Penitentiary (St John the Evangelist Westminster) C 1816-71 microfiche (2001)

PARISH LISTING

ALL HALLOWS, BARKING by the Tower, Great Tower Street (1,761) (united to St Dunstan in the East, 1960)
OR C 1558+, M 1564+, Banns 1852-1960, ML 1977-84, B 1558-1853 (Inc)
BT 1800-01, 1812 (GL)
Cop C 1558-75, M 1564-74 (Ts I, GL); M 1800-12 (Pallot Index); M 1780-1800 (CRW);
Extracts 1558-1850 (Ptd, J. Marskell, 1864); Extr 1565-1744 (Ptd, *Notes & Queries* 3rd ser. 2, 1862 pp.423-5, 3rd ser. 3, 1863 pp.61-2,162-3,323); B 1813-53 (CLBI 3)

ALL HALLOWS, BREAD STREET (336) (Peculiar of the Deanery of the Arches) (united to St John the Evangelist, 1670; united to St Mary le Bow, 1876; closed 1892)
OR C 1538-1892, M 1538-1876, ML 1840-66, B 1538-1851 (CB 1821+, M 1673+ include St John the Evangelist) (GL)
BT 1799, 1802, 1804-11 (LPL); 1813-17, 1819-36, 1851-53 (no M 1813, 1817, 1851-53) (no B 1852-53) (GL)
Cop C 1538-1892, M 1538-1876, B 1538-1851 (Ptd, HS 43, 1913); C 1538-1875 (IGI); M 1538-1837 (Boyd); M 1780-1837 (Pallot Index); B 1813-51 (CLBI)

ALL HALLOWS, HONEY LANE (189) (destroyed 1666; united to St Mary-le-Bow, 1670)
OR C 1538-1697, 1813-92, M 1546-1656, 1664-66, 1818-36, B 1538-1666, 1814-51 (CB 1698-1812, M 1675-1812, Banns 1754-1937 in St Mary le Bow registers) (GL)
BT 1800-02, 1810, 1817-36, 1838-46, 1848-56, 1867 (no M 1817, 1820-24, 1838-67, no B 1817, 1836, 1846-67) (GL)
Cop C 1538-1837 B 1538-1852 (Ptd, HS 44, 1914; index in HS 45, 1915); M 1546-1837 (Ptd, HS 45, 1915); C 1538-1875, M 1546-1656, 1664-66, 1818-36 (IGI); M 1546-1656, 1664-66, 1818-36 (Boyd); M 1780-1837 (Pallot Index); B 1814-51 (CLBI)

ALL HALLOWS, LOMBARD STREET (596) (Peculiar of the Deanery of the Arches) (united to St Benet Gracechurch and St Leonard Eastcheap, 1864; united to St Dionis Backchurch, 1876; united to St Edmund the King and Martyr, 1937; demolished 1939, but tower and furnishings rebuilt in Twickenham)
OR C 1550-1939, M 1553-1939, Banns 1654-62, 1755-1937, B 1549-1853 (GL)
BT 1799, 1803-13 (LPL); 1813-46 (no C 1829, no M 1838-46) (GL)
Cop M 1553-1837 (incl.Banns) (GL: Challen 6); C 1813-46, M 1813-37 (IGI); M 1553-1837 (Boyd); M 1780-1837 (Pallot Index); B 1813-53 (CLBI)

ALL HALLOWS, LONDON WALL (1,861) (united with St Augustine on the Wall alias St Augustine Papey, 1441)
OR C 1559-1875, M 1559-1927, Banns 1823-90, B 1559-1849 (receipts for B 1459-1536) (GL); C 1875+, M 1927+ (Inc)
BT 1629-31, 1639-40, 1801-04, 1807-09, 1811-37 (GL)
Cop CMB 1559-1675 (Ptd, E.B.Jupp and R.Hovenden, 1878); M 1675-1837 (GL: Challen 23); C 1559-1875, M 1559-1880 (IGI); C 1559-1675, 1701-75, 1801-37; M 1780-1837 (Pallot Index); B 1813-49 (CLBI)

ALL HALLOWS, LONDON WALL Spanish and Portuguese Synagogue, Bevis Marks f 1656
OR Z 1764+, M 1690+, B 1657+ (Synagogue); Converts 1809-16 (Jewish Theological Seminary, New York)
Cop M 1690-1837 (Ptd, L.D. Barnett and G.H. Whitehill, 1949); M 1837-1901 (Ptd, L.D. Barnett and G.H. Whitehill, 1973); B 1657-1735 (Ptd, *Jewish Historical Society Miscellanies* 6, 1962); Converts 1809-16 (Ptd, ed. Barnett A. Elzas, New York, 1911, photocopy at Jewish Museum)

ALL HALLOWS, LONDON WALL Poultry Chapel (Independent) (f early 18th century in Camomile Street, All Hallows, the Poultry Chapel was built on the site of the old Poultry Compter, in St Mildred Poultry parish, 1819; it was renamed the City Temple, 1872)
OR C 1702-53, 1781-1837 (PRO: RG 4/4207, 4410); registers 1837-c1940 destroyed by enemy action, 1940
Cop C 1702-1837 (IGI)

ALL HALLOWS STAINING, Mark Lane (577) (demolished apart from the tower and united to St Olave, Hart Street, 1870)
OR C 1642-1870, M 1653-1870, Banns 1754-1812, 1824-70, B 1653-1853 (M 1740-54 very defective, no B 1729-36, 1738-45) (receipts for M 1617-28, B 1491-1628, 1645-1706) (GL)
BT 1800-53 (no M 1838-53) (GL)
Cop C 1642-1870 (Ms I GL); M 1653-1740, 1748-50, 1753 (GL: Challen 12); C 1642-1812, 1754-1870, M 1754-1837 (IGI); M 1653-1740, 1748-50 (Boyd); 1800-08, 1810-37 (Pallot Index); B 1813-53 (CLBI); C 1642-1870, M 1653-1753 (SG)

ALL HALLOWS THE GREAT, All Hallows Lane (588) (destroyed 1666; united to All Hallows the Less, 1670; united to St Michael, Paternoster Royal, 1893)
OR C 1668-1888, M 1671-1890, Banns 1754-1812, 1814-89, ML 1813-97, B 1667-1853 (receipts for B 1616-29) (no M 1723-41) (GL)
BT 1800-04, 1807-52, 1854-65 (no C 1857, no M 1860, 1865, no B 1849-65) (GL)
Cop C 1813-40 (and late Baptisms) (Ts I GL, SG, CRW); C 1668-1812, B 1667-1853 (SG); M 1671-1723, 1741-54 (GL: Challen 9); C 1668-1812, M 1754-99 (IGI); M 1671-1723, 1741-75, 1801-37 (Boyd); M 1800-37 (Pallot Index); B 1813-53 (CLBI)

ALL HALLOWS THE LESS, Thames Street (154) (destroyed 1666; united to All Hallows the Great, 1670; united to St Michael, Paternoster Royal, 1893)
OR C 1558-1812, M 1558-1666, B 1558-1812 (M 1671+, CB 1813+ in All Hallows the Great registers) (GL)
BT 1629-31, 1639-40, 1800-04, 1807-12 (GL)
Cop M 1558-1666 (GL: Challen 9); C 1558-1875 (IGI); M 1558-1666 (Boyd); 1800-37 (Pallot Index)

AUSTIN FRIARS *see* **ST PETER LE POER**

BRIDEWELL Chapel, Bridewell Precinct (456) (extra-parochial; chapel united to St Bride, 1906)
OR C 1670-1863, M 1671-1863, Banns 1757-1862, B 1667-1845 (most of these registers were damaged 1940; some registers were recovered in 1996; post-1863 entries in St Bride registers) (GL)
BT 1665-66, 1813-16, 1818-44, 1846-54, 1856-63 (no M 1813-14, 1816, 1819-21, 1826-27, 1838-63, no B 1846-63) (GL)
Cop C 1670-83, M 1671-93, B 1667-78, Extr B 1678-1780 (C of A: Chester Ms 35); M 1671-93, 1701-25 (Boyd); M 1665-66, 1682-1837 (GL, SG, CRW); B 1813-44 (CLBI 3)

CHRIST CHURCH, GREYFRIARS, Newgate Street (2,622) (created from St Audoen alias St Ewin, St Nicholas Shambles and part of St Sepulchre, 1547, using the old Greyfriars church) (united to St Leonard, Foster Lane, 1670; small part of parish incorporated in St Andrew Undershaft and in St Vedast, with the main part united to St Sepulchre, 1954)
OR B 1275-c1540 (BL: Ms Cotton Vitellius F.XII, pars 14, ff. 273-315); C 1547-88, 1724-1940, M 1547-88, 1837-1940, Banns 1870-1940, B 1547-88 (receipts for B 1593-96) (*see* St Nicholas Shambles for 1538-47); CMB 1588-1666 presumably destroyed, 1666; C 1666-1724, M 1667-1837, B 1666-1940 were destroyed and several surviving registers were severely damaged by enemy action, 1940) (GL)
BT 1800-02, 1804, 1807-36 (no B 1801) (GL)
Cop B 1275-c1540 (Ptd, E.B.S. Shepherd, *Archaeological Journal* 59, 1902, pp.266-287); C 1547-88, 1657-1754, M 1547-88, 1667-1754, B 1538-88, 1666-1754 (Ptd, HS 21, 1895; *see* note in *The Genealogist* NS 12, 1896, pp.223-225); M 1639-40 (GL, SG, CRW); C 1547-1754, 1804-75, M 1542-1753, 1804-80 (IGI); M 1538-88, 1667-1754 (Boyd); M 1780-1837 (Pallot Index); Extr C 1657-1812, M 1667-1778, B 1666-1812 (C of A: Chester 48); Extr C 1669-1877, M 1676-1928, B 1667-1853 (Ms GL); B 1813-53 (CLBI 3)
Cop (Mf) C 1724-1812 (SG)

FLEET PRISON, AND RULES OF THE FLEET (clandestine marriages were performed in the Prison, and in a variety of taverns, etc. in the neighbourhood until prevented by Hardwicke's Marriage Act of 1754; though some of the registers have recently been shown to be forgeries, the several hundred volumes which survive are the most likely source for any marriage not in the expected parish, especially for south-east England and the period c1720-54; *see also* Old Red Hand and Mitre Chapel)
OR M 1667-1754 (PRO: RG 7); M 1725-31 (Bodleian Lib: Ms. Rawlinson B.360)
Cop M 1691-1702 (Ts I GL, SG); Extr M (for entries relating to parts of Kent, Surrey and Sussex) c1700-54 (Ts SG); Extr M 1709-54 (Ptd, J.S. Burn, 1833); Extr (of a very small proportion) M c1667-1754 (Boyd)

GUILDHALL CHAPEL *see* **ST LAWRENCE JEWRY**

HOLY TRINITY MINORIES (508) (united to St Botolph Aldgate, 1893; destroyed, 1940) (a royal Peculiar until 1730; many clandestine marriages c1644-c1713)
OR C 1563-1897, M 1579-1649, 1658-63, 1676-1898, Banns 1754-1898, B 1566-1852 (GL)
BT 1629-30, 1638-40, 1801-04, 1808-48 (no M 1838-48) (GL); CB 1843, 1845 (LMA)
Cop M 1644-48, 1657-83 (Ms GL); C 1563-1875 (IGI); M 1579-1663 (Boyd); M 1799-1837 (Pallot Index); B 1813-52 (CLBI); M 1676-1754 (Ptd Mf, ELFHS, 1988-96)

HOLY TRINITY THE LESS, Little Trinity Lane (443) (destroyed 1666; united to St Michael Queenhithe, 1670; united to St James Garlickhithe, 1875)
OR C 1547-1836, M 1547-1666, 1670-1830, Banns 1754-1812, B 1547-1852 (GL)
BT 1629-31, 1639-40, 1800-05, 1807-19 (GL)
Cop M 1547-1666,1694-96, 1730 (GL: Challen 27, SG); M 1547-1666, 1694-96, 1730 (Boyd); M 1754-1830, Banns 1754-1812 (Ts I GL, SG, CRW); B 1813-52 (CLBI); C 1547-1836 (IGI)

HOLY TRINITY THE LESS Hamburg Lutheran Chapel, Great Trinity Lane
OR C 1694-1836, M 1671-1754, B 1669-1836 (PRO: RG 4/4650)
Cop B 1813-47 (CLBI 3)

LAMB'S CHAPEL *see* **ST OLAVE SILVER STREET**

MERCERS' HALL CHAPEL *see* **ST MARTIN POMEROY**

OLD RED HAND AND MITRE CHAPEL *see* **ST SEPULCHRE**

ST ALBAN, WOOD STREET (582) (united to St Olave Silver Street, 1670; united to St Michael Wood Street and St Mary Staining, 1894; bombed 1940; united to St Vedast, Foster Lane, 1954)
OR C 1662-1786, M 1662-1811, 1903-34, B 1662-1786, 1840-49 (receipts for B 1584-1657, 1661-75; C c1565?-1662, 1786-c1940, M c1565?-1662, 1811-1902, B c1565?-1662, 1786-1849 destroyed by enemy action, 1940) (GL)
BT 1629-30, 1800-52 (no M 1837-52, no B 1850-52) (GL)
Cop Extr C 1591-1623, M 1572, B 1600, 1617 (Ptd, J.P. Malcolm, 1803, *Londonium Redivivum* 2, pp.310-311); CMB 1629-30, CB 1662-1786, C 1800-52, M 1662-1836, B 1800-49 (Ts GL, SG, CRW); C 1662-1786, 1800-52, M 1800-36 (IGI); M 1800-37 (Pallot Index); B 1813-52 (CLBI)

ST ALPHAGE LONDON WALL (alias St Alphage, Sion College) (1,087) (united to St Mary the Virgin, Aldermanbury, 1917; united to St Giles, Cripplegate, 1954)
OR C 1613-1920, M 1613-1916, Banns 1754-1880, 1882, 1885, 1911, B 1613-78, 1699-1851 (receipts for B 1527-1631) (GL)
BT 1629-30, 1639-40, 1800-01, 1803-40, 1842-49 (no M 1837-49) (GL)
Cop M 1613-1837 (Ts I CRW, GL, SG); M 1613-1868 (Ms I GL); C 1813-75, M 1754-1885 (IGI); M 1800-01, 1803-37 (Pallot Index); B 1813-51 (CLBI)
Cop (Mf) C 1813-75 (SG)

ST ANDREW BY THE WARDROBE, St Andrew's Hill, Queen Victoria Street (756) (united to
St Ann Blackfriars, 1670)
OR C 1558-1939, M 1558-1940, Banns 1822-45, ML 1712-1889, B 1558-1850 (GL);
C 1939+, M 1940+ (Inc)
BT 1800-05, 1807-24, 1826-43, 1845-52 (no B 1850-52) (GL)
Cop C 1558-1875, M 1558-1885 (IGI); M 1800-09, 1811-37 (Pallot Index); B 1813-50 (CLBI 3)
Cop (Mf) C 1558-1838, M 1558-1797 (SG)

ST ANDREW HOLBORN, Holborn Viaduct (32,904)
OR C 1558-1889, M 1559-1952, Banns 1653-58, 1754-62, 1862-93, 1900-53, B 1556-1855 (GL);
C 1889+, M 1953+ (Inc)
BT 1639-40, 1833-35 (GL)
Cop C 1558-1875 (IGI); M 1754-64 (Ts SG); M 1780-1837 (Pallot Index); B 1813-55 (CLBI 3)
Cop (Mf) C 1791-1849, M 1774-1838, B 1768-1838 (LMA)

ST ANDREW HOLBORN Fetter Lane Chapel (later Union Road, Leyton, Essex) (Independent)
f 1660
OR C 1730-1837, B 1786-1801 (PRO: RG 4/4236); C 1730-1896 (GLRO: N/C/31/2)

ST ANDREW HOLBORN Great Queen Street Chapel, Lincoln's Inn Fields
(Wesleyan Methodist)
OR C 1812-1909, M 1843-1907, 1912-30, B 1828-56 (LMA)

ST ANDREW HUBBARD (alias St Andrew Budge Row), Eastcheap (354) (destroyed 1666;
united to St Mary at Hill 1670)
OR C 1538-1601, 1621-23, 1706-90 , M 1538-99, 1621-23, Banns 1824-1921, B 1538-99,
1621-23, 1706-90 (receipts for B 1639-53) (GL); C 1813+, M 1837+ (Inc St Mary at Hill)
BT 1639-40, 1800-05, 1807-44, 1846 (no M 1838-44) (GL)
Cop CM 1538-1600 (SG); M 1538-99, 1621-22 (GL: Challen 27); M 1639-40, 1813-1837
(Ts I GL, SG, CRW); C 1538-99, 1706-90, 1800-37, M 1800-37 (IGI); M 1538-1622
(Boyd); M 1812-37 (Pallot Index); B 1813-46 (CLBI)

ST ANDREW UNDERSHAFT, St Mary Axe (1,080) (united to St Mary Axe, 1562)
OR C 1558-1901, M 1558-1970, Banns 1754-60, 1764-85, 1792-1814, 1824-51, ML 1836-58,
1908-61, B 1558-1849 (GL); C 1901+, M 1970+ (Inc)
BT 1639-40, 1800-27, 1829-30, 1833-35 (GL)
Cop M 1558-1837, Banns 1754-60, 1764-85, 1792-1814, 1824-37 (GL: Challen 37);
C 1558-1875 M 1558-1837 (IGI); M 1726-75, 1801-37 (Boyd); M 1780-1837 (Pallot Index);
B 1813-49 (CLBI)

ST ANNE BLACKFRIARS (2,622) (destroyed 1666; united to St Andrew by the Wardrobe 1670)
OR C 1560-1861, M 1562-1726, 1813-49, Banns 1717-24, 1822-45, ML 1712-1889,
B 1566-1849 (M 1726-1812 in St Andrew by the Wardrobe registers) (GL); C 1861+ (Inc
St Andrew by the Wardrobe)
BT 1629-31, 1639-40, 1800-05, 1807-11, 1813-24, 1826-43, 1845-52 (no M 1841-52,
no B 1850-52) (GL)
Cop C 1560-1861 (IGI); M 1801-10, 1813-37 (Pallot Index); B 1813-49 (CLBI 3)
Cop (Mf) M 1726-1812 (SG)

ST ANNE BLACKFRIARS Carter Lane, Blackfriars, later Upper Street Islington (Presbyterian)
f 1708
OR C 1711-51, 1760-1811 (PRO: RG 4/4141, 4231)
Cop C 1711-1811 (IGI)

ST ANNE BLACKFRIARS French Church fl 1710
OR no registers known

ST ANNE BLACKFRIARS Friar Street, Blackfriars (Swedenborgian)
OR C 1787-1837 (PRO: RG 4/4239)
Cop C 1787-1837 (IGI)

ST ANNE AND ST AGNES, Gresham Street, Aldersgate (421) (united to St Vedast, Foster Lane, 1954)
OR C 1640-1924, M 1642-1938, Banns 1774-99, 1824-1920, ML 1831-1937, B 1640-1853 (GL)
BT 1629-30, 1665-66, 1800-01, 1807-50 (no C 1823, 1837, no M 1838-50, no B 1800) (GL)
Cop CMB 1640-1837 (Ms I GL); C 1640-1875, M 1641-1754 (IGI); M 1800-01, 1806-37 (Pallot Index); B 1813-53 (CLBI)

ST ANNE AND ST AGNES Meeting House, Bull and Mouth Street (Society of Friends)

ST ANTHOLIN, Budge Row (356) (demolished 1875, united to St John the Baptist upon Walbrook; united to St Mary Aldermary, 1873)
OR C 1539-1872, M 1539-1873, Banns 1754-1952, B 1539-1853 (GL)
BT 1800-02, 1807-14, 1816-36 (GL)
Cop CMB 1538-1754 (Ptd, HS 8, 1883); C 1754-1840, M 1754-1837, B 1754-1853 (Ts I GL, SG, CRW); C 1538-1872, M 1538-1837 (IGI); M 1538-1754 (Boyd); M 1800-37 (Pallot Index); B 1813-53 (CLBI)

ST AUDOEN (alias **ST EWEN**) (destroyed at dissolution; incorporated in Christ Church Greyfriars, 1547; no known registers)

ST AUGUSTINE ON THE WALL (alias **ST AUGUSTINE PAPEY**), London Wall (united to All Hallows London Wall, 1441)

ST AUGUSTINE, Watling Street (311) (united to St Faith under St Paul's, 1670; bombed 1940; united to St Mary le Bow, 1954)
OR C 1559-1925, M 1559-1940, Banns 1754-1805, 1824-1940, B 1559-1853 (GL)
BT 1629-31, 1800-01, 1807, 1809-45 (no M 1837-45) (GL)
Cop M 1559-1837, Banns 1754-1805 (GL: Challen 13); C 1559-1762, 1769-1875, M 1559-1754 (IGI); M 1559-1775, 1801-36 (Boyd); M 1780-1837 (Pallot Index); B 1813-53 (CLBI)

ST BARTHOLOMEW BY THE ROYAL EXCHANGE (345) (united to St Margaret Lothbury, 1839; demolished 1891)
OR C 1558-1840, M 1559-1706, 1712-1840, Banns 1754-1840, B 1558-1678, 1706-1838 (receipts for B 1703-04; rough entries only of CMB 1712-23) (GL)
BT 1800-12, 1814-32, 1840 (no MB 1840)
Cop M 1559-1754 (GL: Challen 8, SG); M 1754-1837 (Ts I GL, SG, CRW); C 1558-1840, M 1723-1840 (IGI); M 1558-1706, 1712-54 (Boyd); M 1800-37 (Pallot Index); B 1813-38 (CLBI)

ST BARTHOLOMEW THE GREAT, Bartholomew Close, West Smithfield (2,923) (originally Priory church, made parochial, 1544)
OR C 1616-1926, Z 1695-1710, M 1616-1934, Banns 1754-1969, B 1616-1853 (GL); C 1926+, M 1934+ (Inc)
BT 1665-66, 1807-64 (no M 1838-64, no B 1855-64)
Cop B 1554-1884 (Inc); C 1616-1893, M 1616-1914, B 1616-1853 (Ts I GL); C 1616-1875, M 1716-1885 (IGI); M 1807-37 (Pallot Index); B 1813-53 (CLBI 3)

ST BARTHOLOMEW THE GREAT Bartholomew Chapel Bartholomew Close (Independent) now closed
OR C 1740-79, 1827-37 (PRO: RG 4/4134-4135, 4371)
Cop C 1740-79 (IGI)

ST BARTHOLOMEW THE LESS, West Smithfield (863) (chapel in St Bartholomew's Hospital which became parochial, 1547)
OR CM 1547+, B 1547-1853 (The Archivist, St Bartholomew's Hospital, EC1A 7BE)
BT CMB 1629-31, 1639-40, 1807-13 (GL)
Cop C 1547-1894, M 1547-1837, Banns 1754-1941, B 1547-1848 (Ptd, Mf, 1992); M 1547-1837 (GL: Challen 52); M 1807-13, 1820-37 (Pallot Index); D of patients 1762-69, 1807-16, 1826-34 (Ts SG)

ST BARTHOLOMEW THE LESS Hospital Burial Ground, Seward Street
OR B 1744-55, 1846-49 (The Archivist, St Bartholomew's Hospital, EC1A 7BE)
Cop B 1744-55, 1846-49; B 1846-49 (CLBI)

ST BENET FINK, Threadneedle Street (459) (united to St Peter le Poer, 1842; united to
St Michael Cornhill, 1906; demolished 1940)
OR C 1538-1845, M 1538-1845, Banns 1653-62, 1699-1715, 1754-1845, ML 1796-1845,
B 1538-1845 (GL)
BT 1639-40, 1800-02, 1804-18, 1821-34, 1845 (no M 1845) (GL)
Cop M 1538-1845, Banns 1653-62, 1699-1715, 1754-1845 (GL: Challen 7, SG);
C 1538-1845, M 1538-1845 (IGI); M 1538-1775, 1801-36 (Boyd); M 1780-1837 (Pallot
Index); B 1813-45 (CLBI)

ST BENET FINK French Church and Hospital, Threadneedle Street (moved to St Martin
le Grand, 1842; moved to Soho Square, 1893)
OR C 1595-1840, M 1599-1753 (PRO: RG 4/4552-58, 4587-88, 4634, 4643, 4645-46);
C 1840+ (Church)
Cop C 1595-1840, M 1599-1752 (Ptd, Hug Soc 9, 13, 16, 23, 1896-1916);
M 1599-1752 (Boyd); C 1595-1840 (IGI)

ST BENET, GRACECHURCH STREET (348) (united to St Leonard Eastcheap, 1670; united to
All Hallows, Lombard Street, 1864; united to St Edmund the King and Martyr, 1937)
OR C 1559-1866, M 1558-1865, Banns 1754-99, 1824-65, B 1558-1853 (receipts for
B 1548-1653) (GL)
BT 1629-31, 1639-40, 1801-02, 1804, 1807-09, 1811-32, 1836, 1844-64 (no C 1844-45,
no M 1831-32, 1846-64, no B 1854-64) (GL)
Cop M 1558-1837 (GL: Challen 6, SG); C 1730-1866, M 1730-1837 (IGI); M 1558-1837
(Boyd); M 1800-37 (Pallot Index); B 1813-52 (CLBI)

ST BENET, GRACECHURCH STREET Meeting House, Gracechurch Street (Society of
Friends) (registers listed more fully in introduction)
OR Z 1795-1837, M 1795-1836, B 1795-1837 (PRO: RG 6/415-16)
Cop Z 1795-1837, M 1795-1836, B 1795-1837 (Friends' House)

ST BENET PAULS WHARF, Upper Thames Street (612) (now known as the **Welsh Church**)
(united to St Peter, 1670; united to St Nicholas Cole Abbey,1879; Welsh Congregation 1880)
OR C 1619-1877, 1880-1931, M 1619-1879, Banns 1754-91, B 1619-1853 (receipts for
B 1605-57) (GL)
BT 1800-51, 1853-65, 1867-68 (no M 1838-68, no B 1852-68) (GL)
Cop C 1619-1837 (Ptd, HS 38, 1909); M 1619-1730 (Ptd, HS 39, 1910); M 1731-1837 (Ptd, HS
40, 1911); B 1619-1837 (Ptd, HS 41, 1912); C 1838-40, B 1837-53 (Ts I GL, SG, CRW);
C 1619-1875, M 1619-68, 1680-1879 (IGI); M 1619-1837 (Boyd); M 1780-1837 (Pallot
Index); B 1813-53 (CLBI)

ST BENET PAULS WHARF Herald's College, College of Arms, Queen Victoria Street
OR CZ 1747-82 (C of A)

ST BENET SHEREHOG, Pancras Lane (180) (destroyed 1666; united to St Stephen Walbrook,
1670)
OR No early registers survive
BT 1629-31, 1639-40 (GL)
Cop CMB 1629-31, 1639-40 (Ts I GL, SG, CRW)

ST BOTOLPH, ALDERSGATE (3,994)
OR C 1638-1984, M 1640-1953, Banns 1653-64, 1779-1935, ML 1834-1918, B 1640-1853
(very defective receipts for B 1468-1636, 1639-40) (GL)
BT 1801, 1807-09, 1811-47 (GL)
Cop M 1640-1755 (GL: Challen 5); C 1638-1812, M 1640-1812, B 1640-1789 (part I only GL);
C 1640-1844, M 1754-1872 (IGI); M 1640-1755 (Boyd); M 1807-37 (Pallot Index);
B 1813-53 (CLBI 3)

ST BOTOLPH, ALDERSGATE Aldersgate Street (Wesleyan Methodist) f 1826 (formerly St Mary Axe)
OR C 1827-37 (PRO: RG 4/4217)
Cop C 1827-37 (Ts GL)

ST BOTOLPH, ALDERSGATE Hare Court Chapel, Aldersgate Street (Independent) f 1690 closed by 1850
OR C 1820-37 (PRO: RG 4/4368)
Cop C 1820-37 (IGI)

ST BOTOLPH ALDGATE, Aldgate High Street (13,068) (united to Holy Trinity in the Minories, 1893)
OR C 1558-1927, M 1558-1945, Banns 1583-1600, 1653-58, 1754-1878, B 1558-1853 (receipts for B 1547-85) (GL); C 1927+. M 1945+ (Inc)
BT 1802-15 (no CB 1815) (GL)
Cop CMB 1593-1640 (Ms I only GL); C 1558-1875 (IGI); B 1813-53 (CLBI 3)

ST BOTOLPH BILLINGSGATE, Thames Street (207) (destroyed 1666; united to St George Botolph Lane, 1670; united to St Mary at Hill, 1901)
OR C 1685-1891, M 1813-35, ML 1818-88, B 1686-1845 (receipts for B 1603-72, 1678-1739, M in St George Botolph Lane registers) (GL)
BT 1629-31, 1639-40, 1801-09, 1812-53 (GL)
Cop M 1813-35 (GL: Challen 41); C 1629-31, 1639-40, 1685-1840 (and late baptisms), M 1629-31, 1639-40, 1813-35, B 1629-31, 1639-40, 1685-1845 (Ts I GL, SG, CRW; C 1686-1875 (IGI); M 1801-09, 1813, 1815-27, 1829-30, 1833, 1834-36 (Pallot Index); M 1754-1835 (Boyd); B 1813-45 (CLBI)

ST BOTOPH BISHOPSGATE Bishopsgate (10,256)
OR C 1558-1898, M 1558-1958, Banns 1653-60, 1833-1950, ML 1848-73, B 1558-1849, Funeral accounts 1851-67 (GL); C 1898+, M 1958+ (Inc)
BT 1639-40, 1800-62 (no M 1838-62, no B 1854-62) (GL)
Cop C 1558-1690, M 1558-1754, B 1558-1752 (Ptd, A.W.C. Hallen, 3 vols., 1889-95); C 1836-98, M 1754-1837, B 1841-49 (Ms I only GL); C 1558-1862, M 1558-1846 (IGI); M 1558-1754 (Boyd); M 1800-37 (Pallot Index); B 1813-53 (CLBI 3)
Cop (Mf) 1717-41 (SG)

ST BOTOPH BISHOPSGATE Meeting House, Devonshire House, Houndsditch (Society of Friends) (registers listed more fully in introduction)
OR Z 1655-1837, M 1666-1837, B 1719-1837 (PRO: RG 6)
Cop Z 1655-1837, M 1666-1837, B 1719-1837 (Friends' House)

ST BOTOPH BISHOPSGATE Hand Alley, Bishopsgate (from 1729 in New Broad Street) (Presbyterian)
OR C 1705-53, 1760-89 (PRO: RG 4/4138-39)
Cop C 1705-53 (IGI)

ST BOTOPH BISHOPSGATE Meeting House New Broad Street (Independent) f 1727 now closed
OR C 1727-1837 (PRO: RG 4/4376)
Cop C 1727-1837 (IGI)

ST BOTOPH BISHOPSGATE Bishopsgate Street Chapel (became White's Row Chapel, Spitalfields
OR C 1756-1908 (LMA)

ST BOTOPH BISHOPSGATE Parliament Court Chapel, Artillery Street, Bishopsgate, St Botolph Bishopsgate, Middlesex (Baptist)
OR Z 1795-1811 (PRO: RG 4/4369)
Cop Z 1795-1811 (IGI)

ST BRIDE, Fleet Street (7,316) (united to Bridewell and Whitefriars Precincts, 1906)
OR C 1588-1939, 1952, M 1587-1666, 1676-1969, Banns 1735-1825, 1850-1908, ML 1869-72,
    1883-1907, B 1587-1854 (Extr B 1274-1587 taken from testator's intentions) (GL);
    C 1939+, M 1969+ (Inc)
BT 1801-72, 1874 (no M 1839-74, no B 1855-74)
Cop CM 1587-1653, B 1587-95 (GL); C 1587-1736, 1813-59, M 1587-1735, 1775-1810,
    1826-65, 1870-80 (IGI); M 1810-37 (Pallot Index); B 1813-53 (CLBI 3)
Cop (Mf) CM 1587-1653, B 1587-95 (SG)

ST CHRISTOPHER LE STOCKS, Threadneedle Street (72) (closed and united to St Margaret
    Lothbury, 1781, most of site being occupied by the Bank of England)
OR C 1557-1781, Z 1697-1704, M 1557-1780, Banns 1755-80, ML 1775-79, B 1557-1781
    (later registrations at St Margaret Lothbury) (GL)
BT 1664-66 (GL)
Cop 1557-1781 (Ptd, E. Freshfield, 3 vols., 1882); C 1557-1781, M 1558-1780 (IGI);
    M 1557-1780 (Boyd)

ST CLEMENT EASTCHEAP, Clement's Lane (256) (united to St Martin Orgar, 1670)
OR C 1539-1940, M 1539-1839, Banns 1787-1928, B 1539-1853 (GL)
BT 1801-34, 1837-50 (no M 1839-40) (GL)
Cop CM 1539-1839, B 1539-1663 (Ptd, HS 67, 1937); B 1671-1853 (Ptd, HS 68, 1938);
    M 1539-1839, Banns 1787-1830 (GL: Challen 6); C 1539-1877, M 1539-1839 (IGI);
    M 1539-1839 (Boyd); M 1780-1837 (Pallot Index); B 1813-53 (CLBI)

ST DIONIS BACKCHURCH, Lime Street (810) (Peculiar of the Deanery of the Arches)
    (demolished 1876; united to All Hallows, Lombard St. 1876; with St Edmund the King and
    Martyr, 1937)
OR C 1538-1666, 1668-1877, M 1538-1666, 1674-1877, Banns 1754-1877, B 1538-1849 (GL)
BT 1799-1802, 1813 (LPL); 1814-56 (no M 1838-56, no B 1846, 1850-56) (GL)
Cop CMB 1538-1754 (Ptd, HS 3, 1878); M 1754-1837, Banns 1754-1823 (GL: Challen 6);
    C 1538-1877, M 1538-1837 (IGI); M 1538-1837 (Boyd); M 1780-1837 (Pallot Index);
    B 1813-49 (CLBI)

ST DUNSTAN IN THE EAST, St Dunstan's Hill (1,157) (bombed 1940; united to All Hallows
    Barking, 1960)
OR C 1558-1938, 1948, M 1558-1939, Banns 1754-89, 1821-51, B 1558-1853 (receipts for
    B 1495-1506) (GL); M 1944-49, Banns 1852-1926 (Inc All Hallows Barking)
BT 1799-1800, 1804, 1806-10, 1812-14, 1837-38 (LPL); 1815-16, 1846-52,
    1854-56, 1858-59 (no M 1846-59, no B 1854-59) (GL)
Cop CMB 1558-1653 (Ptd, HS 69, 1939); CMB 1653-1691 (Ptd, HS 84-85, 1955);
    C 1692-1758, M 1692-1754, B 1692-1766 (Ptd, HS 86-87, 1958); M 1605-25 (Ptd,
    The Genealogist NS 11 pp.36-47, 1895); C 1766-c1860, M 1754-1837, B 1766-1853
    (Ms I only GL); Extr C 1818-20, 1841-44, 1859-66, 1909-16 (Ms GL); C 1558-1758,
    1766-1816, M 1558-1880 (IGI); C 1816-1938 (GL); M 1605-25 (Boyd); M 1799-1837 (Pallot
    Index); B 1813-53 (CLBI)

ST DUNSTAN IN THE WEST, Fleet Street (3,443)
OR C 1558-1990, M 1560-1970, Banns 1653-59, 1754-57, 1811-41, 1891-1959,
    ML 1731-1884, B 1558-1856, 1927, D 1879-81, 1884-86 (receipts for B 1516-1608) (GL)
BT 1639-40, 1800-43, 1845-46, 1848-49 (no C 1803, 1806, no M 1838-49) (GL)
Cop C 1771-1836, M 1779-1837, B 1813-56 (Ms part I only GL); C 1800-40, M 1800-37
    (IGI); M 1701-75 (Boyd); M 1800-37 (Pallot Index); Extr C 1601-49, M 1602-1762,
    B 1650-1777 (SG); B 1813-56 (CLBI 3)

ST EDMUND KING and MARTYR, Lombard Street (382) (united to St Nicholas Acons, 1670; united to All Hallows Lombard Street, St Benet Gracechurch, St Leonard Eastcheap and St Dionis Backchurch, 1937)
OR C 1670-1980, M 1673-1982, Banns 1811-79, 1881-1980, B 1670-1853 (GL)
BT 1800-03, 1807-45, 1847-60 (no C 1850, no M 1838-60, no B 1851-60) (GL)
Cop C 1670-1812, M 1673-1812, B 1670-1789 (Ptd, W. Briggs, 1892); C 1813-40, M 1813-37, B 1813-50 (Ts I GL, SG, CRW); C 1670-1875, M 1673-1837 (IGI); M 1670-1812 (Boyd); M 1780-99, 1812-37 (Pallot Index); B 1813-50 (CLBI)

ST ETHELBURGA, BISHOPSGATE (665) (part united to St Helen Bishopsgate, part to St Botolph Bishopsgate, 1954; destroyed by terrorist action, 1993)
OR C 1671-1974, M 1679-1951, Banns 1809-23, 1865-1953, B 1672-1839 (receipts for B 1569-1681) (GL)
BT 1800-50 (no Jan-Apr 1805, Jun-Dec 1806, no M 1838-50, no B 1845-50) (GL)
Cop C 1671-1914, M 1679-1754, 1792-1915, B 1672-1849 (Ptd, W.J. Cobb, 1915; this edition gives only names and years); M 1754-92 (Ts I GL, SG, CRW); C 1671-1873, M 1671-1885 (IGI); M 1679-1754, 1792-1837 (Boyd); M 1800-37 (Pallot Index); B 1813-49 (CLBI 3)

ST EWEN *see* **ST AUDOEN**

ST FAITH UNDER ST PAUL'S (841) (this church was located under the choir of St Paul's Cathedral; destroyed in 1666 it was not rebuilt in the new Cathedral; united to St Augustine, Watling Street, 1670; united to St Mary le Bow, 1954)
OR C 1645-1900, M 1690-91, 1695-98, 1813-37, B 1645-1853 (M 1674-1812 in registers of St Augustine) (GL)
BT 1813-52 (no C 1846, no M 1837-52) (GL)
Cop M 1813-37 (GL: Challen 13, SG); C 1645-1875 (IGI); M 1813-37 (Boyd; but listed as St Augustine); M 1780-1837 (Pallot Index); B 1813-53 (CLBI)

ST FAITH UNDER ST PAUL'S Wesleyan Methodists' Metropolitan Registry, Paternoster Row
OR ZC 1808-38 (PRO: RG 4/4677-80)

ST GABRIEL FENCHURCH STREET (355) (destr. 1666; united to St Margaret Pattens, 1670)
OR C 1571-1901, M 1572-1684, 1814-37, B 1571-1851 (C 1901-52, M 1684-1812, 1837-1952, Banns 1754-1881 in St Margaret Pattens registers) (GL)
BT 1801, 1803-05, 1807-12 (GL)
Cop M 1572-1684, 1814-37 (Ts I GL, SG, CRW); C 1571-1872, M 1572-1683 (IGI); M 1814-37 (Pallot Index); B 1813-51 (CLBI)

ST GEORGE, BOTOLPH LANE (229) (united to St Botolph by Billingsgate 1670; demolished 1876; united to St Mary at Hill, 1901)
OR C 1548-1891, M 1547-1890, Banns 1580-95, 1654-60, 1754-1842, ML 1818-88, B 1546-1848 (B 1390-1546 compiled from monumental inscriptions, 1574) (GL)
BT 1801-09, 1812-53 (GL)
Cop M 1547-1837 (GL: Challen 41); M 1653-60, 1685-1720 (SG); M 1547-1837 (Boyd); C 1813-75, M 1754-1885 (IGI); M 1800-08, 1812-37 (Pallot Index); B 1813-48 (CLBI)
Cop (Mf) C 1813-75 (SG)

ST GILES without CRIPPLEGATE, Fore Street (13,134) (until 1723 this parish was partially in the City of London (which part was known as the Freedom), partially in Middlesex (which part was known as the Lordship); in that year, the Middlesex part was made into the parish of St Luke Old Street) (united to St Alphage London Wall, 1954; united to St Luke Old Street, the Charterhouse and the Liberty of Glasshouse Yard, 1966)
OR C 1561-1961, M 1561-1953, 1963-87, Banns 1782-86, 1791-1832, 1838-1940, 1976-82, B 1561-1853, Funeral accounts 1854-1929, Interment of ashes 1929 (GL); C 1961+, M 1987+ (Inc)
BT 1813-37, 1839 (no M 1839) (GL)
Cop C 1561-1875, M 1561-1702 (IGI); M 1561-1625 (Boyd); M 1813-37 (Pallot Index); B 1813-53 (CLBI 3)
Cop (Mf) C 1627-40 (SG)

ST GILES without CRIPPLEGATE Aldermanbury Postern (Independent) closed by 1850
OR C 1730-1837 (PRO: RG 4/4216, 4292, 4418)

ST GILES without CRIPPLEGATE General Registry of births (Dr Williams's Library,
Red Cross Street f 1742 (the main recording place for dissenters)
OR Z 1742-1837 (PRO: RG 4/4666-76; parchment certificates RG 5)

ST GILES without CRIPPLEGATE Jewin Street (Independent) f 1762 moved to Harrow, 1905
OR C 1789-1837 (PRO: RG 4/4273)
Cop C 1789-1837 (IGI)

ST GILES without CRIPPLEGATE Barbican Chapel (Independent) f 1784 now closed
OR C 1776-1822, 1829-57 (PRO: RG 4/4218, 4220, 4370)
Cop C 1776-1837 (IGI)

ST GILES without CRIPPLEGATE Paul's Alley (Baptist)
OR B 1716-18 (GL)

ST GILES without CRIPPLEGATE Princes Street Chapel, Wilson Street Chapel and City
Chapel, Milton Street (Independent) f 1798
OR C 1798-1815, 1818-19 (PRO: RG 4/4407, 4507)
Cop C 1798-1819 (IGI)

ST GILES without CRIPPLEGATE Welsh Chapel, Jewin Street Crescent (Calvinistic Methodist)
f 1770
OR C 1799-1837 (PRO: RG 4/4400)
Cop C 1799-1837 (IGI)

ST GILES without CRIPPLEGATE Jewin Street (Free Thinking Christians) *fl.* 1818-50

ST GILES without CRIPPLEGATE Founders' Hall Chapel *see* **ST MARGARET LOTHBURY**

ST GILES without CRIPPLEGATE Fletchers' Chapel *see* **ST STEPHEN COLEMAN STREET**

ST GILES without CRIPPLEGATE Albion Chapel, Moorgate (Presbyterian) f 1816
OR ZC 1817-37 (PRO: RG 4/4406)
Cop C 1817-37 (IGI)

ST GREGORY BY ST PAUL'S (1,456) (St Gregory's was physically attached to the old
St Paul's Cathedreal; destroyed, 1666 it was not rebuilt; united to St Mary Magdalene Old
Fish Street, 1670; united to St Martin Ludgate, 1890)
OR C 1559-1882, M 1559-1641, 1660-1867, Banns 1754-78, ML 1687-1834, B 1559-1853 (GL)
BT 1813-21 (GL)
Cop M 1559-1754 (GL: Challen 11); CMB 1813-21 (Ts I GL, SG, CRW; M 1559-1700 (SG);
C 1599-1686, 1813-21, M 1559-1687, 1813-21 (IGI); M 1559-1754 (Boyd); M 1800-37
(Pallot Index); B 1813-21 (CLBI)

ST HELEN, Bishopsgate (692) (united to St Martin Outwich, 1873)
OR C 1575-1981, M 1575-1870, Banns 1754-77, 1795-1821, 1824-77, B 1575-1853
(receipts for B 1565-1654) (GL); M 1870+ (Inc)
BT 1813-81 (no M 1840-81, no B 1854-81) (GL)
Cop CMB 1575-1837, Banns 1754-77 (Ptd, HS 31, 1904); B 1837-53 (Ts I GL, SG, CRW);
C 1575-1837, 1844-75, M 1575-1870 (IGI); M 1575-1837 (Boyd); M 1780-1837 (Pallot
Index); B 1813-53 (CLBI)

ST JAMES DUKE'S PLACE (805) (demolished and united to St Katherine
Creechurch, 1873; many clandestine marriages in seventeenth and early eighteenth centuries)
OR C 1747-1872, M 1664-68, 1679-1868, Banns 1772-1817, 1824-54, B 1747-1853
(receipts for B 1728-29, 1736-39, 1743-60) (GL)
BT 1800-04, 1807-10, 1812, 1814 (GL)
Cop M 1664-68, 1679-1837 (Ptd, Phillimore 1-4, 1900-02); C 1747-1840, B 1747-1853
(Ts I GL, SG, CRW; C 1747-1872, M 1664-1700, 1700-1868 (IGI); M 1664-1837 (Boyd);
M 1800-37 (Pallot Index); B 1813-53 (CLBI)

ST JAMES DUKE'S PLACE Great Synagogue, Duke Street f 1690, destroyed 1941
OR C 1770-1887, M 1791-1973, B 1791-1872 (Office of Chief Rabbi)
Cop M 1791-1850 (SG)

ST JAMES GARLICKHITHE, Garlick Hill, Upper Thames Street (637)
(united to St Michael Queenhithe and Holy Trinity the Less, 1875)
OR C 1535-1693, 1708-1971, M 1535-1693, 1708-1868, Banns 1754-1816, 1823-52, 1950,
ML 1810-1933, B 1535-1693, 1708-1853 (GL)
BT 1630-31, 1639-40, 1800-45, 1847-51, 1853-60, 1862-65, 1876, 1881-90 (no M 1876,
1881-90, no B 1854-90) (GL)
Cop CMB 1535-38 (Ptd, W.D. Cooper, *London and Middlesex Archaeological Society
Transactions* 3, 1870, pp.392-396); M 1535-1692, 1708-54 (GL: Challen 27); M 1754-1837,
Banns 1754-73 (Ts I GL, SG, CRW); C 1535-1864, M 1754-1868 (IGI); M 1708-54 (Boyd);
M 1780-1837 (Pallot Index); B 1813-53 (CLBI)

ST JAMES IN THE WALL *see* **ST OLAVE SILVER STREET**

ST JOHN THE BAPTIST upon Walbrook (411) (destroyed 1666; united to St Antholin,
Budge Row, 1670; united to St Mary Aldermary, 1873)
OR C 1682, 1686-1812, B 1686-1812 (receipts for B 1595-1680) (M 1670+, CB 1813+ with
St Antholin) (GL)
BT 1629-30, 1800-05, 1807, 1809-12 (GL)
Cop C 1682-1754, B 1682-1754 (Ptd, HS 8, 1883); C 1754-1812, B 1754-1812
(Ts I GL, SG, CRW); C 1682-1812 (IGI)

ST JOHN THE EVANGELIST (formerly St Werburga), Friday Street (106) (Peculiar of the
Deanery of the Arches) (destroyed 1666; united to All Hallows, Bread Street, 1670; united to
St Mary le Bow, 1876)
OR C 1653-1821, M 1653-66, B 1653-1822 (C 1821+, M 1666+, B 1822+ in registers of
All Hallows Bread Street) (GL)
BT 1799, 1802, 1804-11 (LPL); 1813-16 (GL)
Cop C 1653-1821, M 1563-66, B 1653-1822 (Ptd, HS 43, 1913); C 1653-1821 (IGI);
M 1653-66 (Boyd); B 1813-22 (CLBI)

ST JOHN ZACHARY, Maiden Lane (241) (destroyed 1666; united to St Anne & St Agnes, 1670;
united to St Vedast, Foster Lane, 1954)
OR C 1693-1895, M 1755-1849, Banns 1755-65, B 1693-1849 (receipts for B 1591-1723) (GL)
BT 1665-66, 1800-01, 1807-46, 1848-50 (no M 1838-50, no B 1846, 1848, 1850) (GL)
Cop C 1693-1837, B 1693-1937 (Ms I GL); M 1665-66, 1755-1837 (Ts I GL, SG, CRW);
C 1693-1875, M 1750-1837 (IGI); B 1813-49 (CLBI)

ST KATHERINE COLEMAN, Fenchurch Street (650) (closed for rebuilding, 1738-41; united
to St Olave, Hart Street, 1921)
OR C 1559-1914, M 1563-1738, 1741-1920, Banns 1653-56, 1754-1916, ML 1760-1872,
B 1559-1742, 1813-53 (receipts for B 1734-1833) (GL)
BT 1629-31, 1665-67, 1802, 1807-10, 1812-52 (no M 1838-52) (GL)
Cop M 1563-1754 (GL: Challen 12, SG); C 1710-1876, M 1741-1876 (IGI);
M 1563-1754 (Boyd); B 1813-53 (CLBI)

ST KATHERINE COLEMAN Hambro Synagogue, Church Row alias Magpye Alley, Fenchurch
 Street, f 1707 demolished 1892, and rebuilt in Whitechapel
OR C 1770-1905, M 1797-1938, B 1797-1872 (Office of Chief Rabbi)

ST KATHERINE CREECHURCH, Leadenhall Street (1,718) (united to St James Duke's Place,
 1873)
OR 1663-1947, M 1663-1933, Banns 1812-16, 1824-35, 1874-1950, ML 1780-1805, 1876-99,
 B 1663-1853, Funerals 1853-70 (receipts for B 1650-61) (GL); C 1947+, M 1933+ (Inc)
BT 1639-40, 1664-65, 1800, 1803-63 (M 1804 defective, no M 1838-63, no B 1854-63) (GL)
Cop M 1639-40, 1663-1837 (Ts I GL, SG, CRW); C 1663-1875, M 1663-1885 (IGI); M 1800-37
 (Pallot Index); B 1813-53 (CLBI 3)

ST KATHERINE CREECHURCH New Synagogue, Leadenhall Street f 1761, moved to
 Egerton Road, Stamford Hill, 1915
OR C 1774-1896, M 1790-1823, 1837-1992, B 1810-72 (Office of Chief Rabbi)

ST LAURENCE POUNTNEY, Laurence Pountney Lane (372) (destroyed 1666; united to
 St Mary Abchurch, 1670)
OR C 1538-1907, M 1539-1666, 1813-37, Banns 1654-59, 1757-62, 1804-1911, B 1538-1850
 (receipts for B 1530-49, 1619-81; for M 1670-1812 *see* St Mary Abchurch) (GL); C 1907+
 (Inc St Mary Abchurch)
BT 1629-31, 1639-40, 1802-06, 1808-21, 1823 (no Jan-Mar 1803, May-Sep 1804, Jun-Dec 1806)
 (GL)
Cop M 1538-1666, 1813-37 (GL: Challen 13, SG); M 1538-1666, 1812-37 (Boyd);
 M 1754-1837 (Pallot Index); B 1813-53 (CLBI)
Cop (Mf) C 1813-1907, M 1837-1953, B 1813-50 (GL)

ST LAWRENCE JEWRY, Gresham Street (756) (united to St Mary Magdalene, Milk Street,
 1670; united to St Michael Bassishaw, 1897)
OR C 1538-1812, 1941-53, M 1538-1928, 1938-51, 1957-83, Banns 1754-62, 1764-1873,
 1875-1933, B 1538-1853 (C 1813-1940, M 1928-38 destroyed 1940) (GL); M 1928-38
 (duplicate at London City Reg. Office, Finsbury Town Hall); C 1953+, M 1983+ (Inc)
BT 1800-03, Apr 1805-Apr 1806, 1807-25, 1837-42, 1845-46 (no M 1838-46) (GL)
Cop CMB 1538-1676 (Ptd, HS 70, 1940); CMB 1677-1812 (Ptd, HS 71, 1941); C 1813-25,
 1837-42, M 1813-37, B 1813-53 (Ts I GL, SG, CRW); Extr C 1880, 1908 (Ms GL);
 C 1538-1812, M 1538-1880 (IGI); M 1538-1764 (Boyd); M 1764-1837 (Pallot Index);
 B 1813-53 (CLBI)

ST LAWRENCE JEWRY Guildhall Chapel demolished 1822
OR no registers known to exist, registrations were probably entered at St Lawrence Jewry

ST LEONARD EASTCHEAP (110) (destroyed 1666; united to St Benet Gracechurch, 1670;
 united to All Hallows Lombard Street, 1864; united to St Edmund King and Martyr, 1937)
OR C 1538-1812, M 1538-1705, B 1538-1812 (CB 1813+, M 1705+ *see* St Benet Gracechurch)
 (GL)
BT 1802, 1804-05, 1807-12 (LPL)
Cop M 1538-1705 (GL: Challen 6, SG); C 1538-1812, M 1538-1705 (IGI); M 1538-1705 (Boyd)

ST LEONARD EASTCHEAP King's Weight House Chapel, Fish Street Hill (Independent)
 f 1662, reb 1834, demolished 1883, reb in Duke Street, Grosvenor Square 1891; closed 1966
OR C 1738-75, 1779-1837 (PRO: RG 4/4237, 4394-95, 4500); C 1829-1960 (Dr William's
 Library)
Cop C 1738-1840 (IGI); M 1745-53 (Ptd, *Miscellanea Genealogica et Heraldica* 2nd series 3,
 p.396, 1890)
see The History of the King's Weigh House Church (E. Kaye, 1968)

ST LEONARD FOSTER LANE (220) (destroyed 1666; united to Christ Church Greyfriars,
 1670; united to St Sepulchre, 1954)
OR No early registers survive; *see* Christ Church, Greyfriars
BT 1639-40, 1800-02, 1804, 1808-36 (GL)

ST MAGNUS THE MARTYR, Lower Thames Street (113) (united to St Margaret
New Fish Street, 1670; united to St Michael Crooked Lane, 1831)
OR C 1561-1978, M 1558-1837, Banns 1754-57, 1793-1952, ML 1827-1900, B 1561-1853 (GL);
C 1978+, M 1837+ (Inc)
BT 1800-50 (no M 1838-41) (GL)
Cop M 1558-1712 (GL: Challen 7, SG); M 1712-1837, Banns 1754-57, 1793-1837
(GL: Challen 22); C 1561-1891, M 1558-1891, B 1561-1853 (Ms I only GL); C 1800-50,
M 1800-50 (IGI); M 1557-1775, 1801-37 (Boyd); B 1813-53 (CLBI)

ST MARGARET LOTHBURY (252) (united to St Christopher le Stocks, 1781; united to
St Bartholomew by Royal Exchange, 1839; united to St Olave Old Jewry, St Martin
Pomeroy, St Mildred Poultry and St Mary Colechurch, 1886)
OR C 1558-1924, M 1558-1837, Banns 1774-1899, 1945, ML 1753-1918, 1971, B 1558-1853
(GL); C 1924+, M 1837+ (Inc)
BT 1665-66, 1800-02, 1807-55 (no M 1841-55, no B 1854-55) (GL)
Cop M 1558-1754 (GL: Challen 8, SG); M 1754-1837 (Ts I GL, SG, CRW); C 1558-1774,
1781-1875, M 1558-1837 (IGI); M 1558-1754 (Boyd); M 1800-37 (Pallot Index); B 1813-53
(CLBI)

ST MARGARET LOTHBURY Scots Church, Founders' Hall, north end of Founders.' Court
(moved to London Wall, St Giles Cripplegate, 1764; became Trinity Presbyterian Church,
Canonbury, Islington, 1856)
OR C 1689-1802, 1837-82, 1901-28, M 1909-13, D 1899-1916 (GL); C 1803-40
(PRO: RG 4/4404); C 1822-36, M 1917-35 (United Reformed Church Lib)
Cop C 1702-71 (IGI)

ST MARGARET MOSES, Friday Street (199) (destroyed 1666; united to St Mildred,
Bread Street, 1670)
OR C 1559-1812, M 1558-1665, 1813-39, B 1558-1853 (C 1814-1938, M 1837-1939 destroyed
by enemy action, 1940; M 1670-1812, Banns 1754-74 *see* St Mildred Bread Street) (GL);
C 1938+ (Inc)
BT 1665-66, 1800-29, 1832-42 (no CB 1813, 1829, no M 1665-66, 1838-42) (GL)
Cop C 1559-1837, M 1558-1666, 1813-39, B 1558-1850 (Ptd, HS 42, 1912); C 1559-1836,
1838-42, M 1558-1666, 1813-39 (IGI); M 1557-1666 (Boyd); B 1813-50 (CLBI)

ST MARGARET, NEW FISH STREET (167) (destroyed 1666; united to St Magnus the Martyr,
1670)
OR receipts for B 1577-1678 (no other early registers: *see* St Magnus the Martyr) (GL)
BT 1629-31, 1639-40 (GL)
Cop C 1629-31, 1639-40 (Ts I GL, SG, CRW)

ST MARGARET PATTENS, Rood Lane, Eastcheap (181) (united to St Gabriel Fenchurch, 1670)
OR C 1559-1952, M 1559-1952, Banns 1653-57, 1754-1881, B 1558-1853 (GL)
BT 1800-01, 1803-04, 1807-33, 1840 (no Apr-Dec 1810, no C 1803-04, no M (St Gabriel) 1832,
no M 1840, no B 1803-04) (GL)
Cop M 1650-1837, Banns 1653-57 (Ts I GL, SG, CRW); C 1559-1875, M 1559-1754 (IGI);
M:1559-1660 (Boyd); M 1754-1837 (Pallot Index); B 1813-53 (CLBI)

ST MARTIN LE GRAND (a collegiate church of secular canons f 1056; a Liberty and
extra-parochial precinct; church pulled down, 1548 and New Rents erected; retained
privileges until 1815 when incorporated, partially in St Anne and St Agnes Aldersgate,
partially in St Leonard Foster Lane when the new General Post Office was ordered and which
was built (1825-29) over the entire area of the liberty so that it no longer had a resident
population; earlier, inhabitants had mainly used St Anne and St Agnes)

ST MARTIN LUDGATE, Ludgate Hill (1,185) (united to St Mary Magdalene Old Fish Street and St Gregory by St Paul's, 1890)
OR C 1539-1929, M 1538-1953, Banns 1754-1958, B 1538-1848, Funeral accounts 1848-50, Funeral 1909 (GL); C 1929+, M 1953+ (Inc)
BT 1629-30, 1639-40, 1800-72 (no M 1838-72, no B 1849-72) (GL)
Cop M 1538-1754 (GL: Challen 12); M 1754-1837 (Ts I GL, SG, CRW); C 1538-1875 (IGI); M 1626-1700 (Boyd); M 1800-37 (Pallot Index); B 1813-53 (CLBI 3)

ST MARTIN ORGAR, St Martin's Lane (367) (destroyed 1666; united to St Clement, 1670)
OR C 1625-1812, M 1625-87, 1734, 1738, B 1624-1812 (CB 1813+, M 1688+ in registers of St Clement Eastcheap) (GL)
BT 1629-31, 1639-40, 1801-08 (no M 1801-08) (GL)
Cop C 1625-1812, M 1625-1738, B 1624-1812 (Ptd, HS 68, 1938); M 1625-1738 (GL: Challen 6); M 1625-1738 (IGI); M 1625-1726 (Boyd); M 1780-1838 (Pallot Index)

ST MARTIN ORGAR French Church, Martin's Lane f 1686 closed c1823
OR C 1698-1762, M 1698-1751 (PRO: RG 4/4586)
Cop C 1698-1762, M 1698-1751 (Ptd, Hug Soc 37, 1935); M 1698-1751 (Boyd); C 1698-1762, M 1698-1751 (IGI)

ST MARTIN OUTWICH, Bishopsgate Street (245) (demolished 1796; united to St Helen, Bishopsgate, 1873; sold 1874)
OR C 1670-1873, M 1670-1872, Banns 1755-76, 1824-72, ML 1716, 1817-50, B 1670-1852 (receipts for B 1632-1742) (GL)
BT 1664-65, 1802-33 (GL)
Cop C 1670-1873, M 1670-1872, Banns 1755-76, 1824-72, B 1670-1852 (Ptd, HS 32, 1905); CMB 1664-65 (Ts I GL, SG, CRW); C 1670-1873, M 1670-1872 (IGI); M 1670-1837 (Boyd); M 1780-1837 (Pallot Index); B 1813-52 (CLBI)

ST MARTIN POMEROY, Ironmonger Lane (218) (destroyed 1666; united to St Olave Jewry, 1670; united to St Mildred Poultry and St Mary Colechurch, 1871; united to St Margaret Lothbury, St Christopher le Stocks and St Bartholomew by Royal Exchange, 1886)
OR C 1539-1885, Z 1690-97, M 1539-1648, B 1539-1847 (C 1886+ in registers of St Margaret Lothbury; M 1670+ and Banns 1771+ in registers of St Olave Old Jewry) (GL)
BT 1801, 1807-12 (no M) (GL)
Cop M 1539-1648 (GL: Challen 8, SG); C 1539-1874, M 1539-1647 (IGI); M 1539-1647 (Boyd); M 1800-37 (Pallot Index); B 1813-47 (CLBI)

ST MARTIN POMEROY Mercers' Hall Chapel, Ironmonger Lane (Anglican)
OR M 1641-1754, B 1640-1833 (PRO: RG 4/4436) (several entries for this chapel appear in the registers of St Mary Colechurch, St Mildred Poultry and St Mary le Bow)
Cop M 1701-54 (Boyd); 1641-1833 (C of A); B 1814-33 (CLBI 3)

ST MARTIN VINTRY, Thames Street (226) (destroyed 1666; united to St Michael, Paternoster Royal, 1670; united to All Hallows the Great and All Hallows the Less, 1893)
OR C 1617-65, 1670-1906, M 1617-64, 1675-1710, 1813-36, B 1617-64, 1668-1849 (entries 1617-64 very defective; for M 1702-1812, 1837+, Banns 1754+, ML 1809+ see St Michael, Paternoster Royal) (GL)
BT 1629-31, 1639-40, 1800-01, 1804, 1807-54 (no M 1837-49, no B 1850-54) (GL)
Cop C 1617-1840, M 1617-48, B 1617-1850 (SG); CMB 1617-49 (Ms GL); M 1669-1836 (Ts GL); M 1617-49, 1675-1710 (GL: Challen 9); C 1629-31, 1639-40, 1813-40, MB 1629-31, 1639-40 (Ts I GL, SG, CRW); C 1617-1874, M 1617-49, 1675-1710, 1813-36 (IGI); M 1675-1710 (Boyd); M 1780-1837 (Pallot Index); B 1813-49 (CLBI)

ST MARY ABCHURCH, Abchurch Lane, Cannon Street (501) (united to St Laurence Pountney, 1670)
OR C 1558-1978, M 1558-1953, Banns 1757-62, 1804-1911, B 1558-1851 (GL); CB 1813+, M 1837+ (Inc)
BT May 1802-Apr 1804, Nov 1805-Nov 1806, 1807-21, 1823 (GL)
Cop M 1558-1737 (GL: Challen 5); M 1737-1837, Banns 1757-62 (GL: Challen 13); C 1558-1837, M 1559-1837 (IGI); M 1558-1775, 1801-37 (Boyd); M 1800-37 (Pallot Index); B 1813-53 (CLBI)

ST MARY THE VIRGIN, ALDERMANBURY (789) (united to St Alphage London Wall, 1917; bombed 1940; the ruins sent to U.S.A. and rebuilt there)
OR C 1538-1940, M 1538-1940, Banns 1754-1940, ML 1837-1928, B 1538-1859 (GL)
BT 1800-02, 1804, 1807-36 (GL)
Cop C 1538-1670, M 1538-1666, B 1538-1665 (Ptd, HS 61, 1931); C 1662-1722, M 1667-1721, B 1665-1722 (Ptd, HS 62, 1932); C 1722-1837, M 1722-1837, B 1722-1859 (Ptd, HS 65, 1935); C 1838-40 (Ts GL, SG, CRW); 1538-1877, M 1538-1880 (IGI); M 1701-21, 1751-75, 1801-37 (Boyd); M 1780-1837 (Pallot Index); B 1813-59 (CLBI)

ST MARY ALDERMARY, Bow Lane, Queen Victoria Street (507) (Peculiar of the Deanery of the Arches) (united to St Thomas Apostle, 1670; united to St Antholin and St John the Baptist upon Walbrook, 1873)
OR C 1558-1910, M 1558-1940, Banns 1771-1952, ML 1860-1909, B 1558-1851 (GL); C 1910+, M 1940+ (Inc)
BT 1799-1813 (LPL); 1813-50 (no M 1837-50) (GL)
Cop CMB 1558-1754 (Ptd, HS 5, 1880); C 1754-1840, M 1754-1837, B 1754-1851 (Ts I GL, SG, CRW); C 1558-1875, M 1558-1836 (IGI); M 1558-1754 (Boyd); M 1800-37 (Pallot Index); B 1813-51 (CLBI)

ST MARY AT HILL, St Mary at Hill, Eastcheap (762) (united to St Andrew Hubbard, 1670; united to St George Botolph Lane and St Botolph Billingsgate, 1901)
OR C 1558-1988, M 1559-1837, Banns 1754-1813, 1824-1921, B 1558-1850 (GL); C 1988+, M 1837+ (Inc)
BT 1800-44, 1846 (no M 1838-44) (GL)
Cop M 1559-1754 (GL: Challen 27); C 1558-1750, M 1558-1702, B 1558-1805 (Ms SG, Bpsgate Lib); C 1558-1837, M 1754-1837 (Ts I CRW, GL, SG); M 1560-1837 (IGI); M 1701-54 (Boyd); M 1800-37 (Pallot Index); B 1813-50 (CLBI)

ST MARY AXE, St Mary Axe (united to St Andrew Undershaft, 1562)
OR No early registers known; entries were probably made at St Andrew Undershaft

ST MARY BOTHAW, Turnwheel Lane (253) (Peculiar of the Deanery of the Arches) (destroyed 1666; united to St Swithin, London Stone, 1670; to St Stephen, Walbrook, 1954)
OR C 1536-1654, M 1536-1658, 1754-1812, Banns 1754-64, B 1537-1654 (C 1675-1944, M 1672-1754, 1813-1941, Banns 1778-1852, B 1670-1853 at St Swithin London Stone) (GL)
BT 1799-1802, 1804, 1808-11 (LPL)
Cop M 1536-1658, 1754-1812, Banns 1754-64 (GL: Challen 31); C 1536-1653 (IGI); M 1754-75, 1801-12 (Boyd); M 1804, 1808-11 (Pallot Index)
Cop (Mf) C 1536-1653, M 1536-1657, 1754-1812, B 1536-1653 (SG)

ST MARY COLECHURCH, Cheapside (274) (destroyed 1666; united to St Mildred Poultrey, 1670; united to St Olave, Old Jewry and St Martin Pomeroy, 1871; united to St Margaret Lothbury, St Christopher le Stocks and St Bartholomew by Royal Exchange, 1886)
OR C 1558-1812, M 1558-1666, B 1558-1666, 1671-1812 (CB 1813+, M 1670+ at St Mildred Poultry) (GL)
BT 1629-31, 1665-66, 1800, 1802-04, 1807-10 (GL)
Cop M 1558-1666, 1684 (GL: Challen 8); C 1558-1812 (IGI); M 1558-1666, 1684 (Boyd)

ST MARY LE BOW, Cheapside (376) (Peculiar of the Deanery of the Arches) (united to
St Pancras Soper Lane and All Hallows Honey Lane, 1670; united to All Hallows Bread
Street and St John the Evangelist, 1876; united to St Augustine, St Gregory by St Paul's,
St Faith under St Paul's, St Mildred Bread Street and St Margaret Moses, 1954)
OR C 1538-1631, 1653-1992, M 1538-1631, 1675-1992, Banns 1754-1937, B 1538-1631,
1653-1852 (GL); M 1837+ (Inc)
BT 1799-1808, 1812 (LPL); 1817-46, 1848-56, 1858-62, 1867 (no M 1839-67, no B 1853-67)
(GL)
Cop C 1538-1837, B 1538-1852 (Ptd, HS 44, 1914); M 1538-1837, Banns 1754-1837
(Ptd, HS 45, 1915); C 1538-1837, M 1538-1631, 1697-1836 (IGI); M 1538-1631, 1675-1837
(Boyd); M 1780-1837 (Pallot Index); B 1813-52 (CLBI)

ST MARY MAGDALENE, MILK STREET (288) (destroyed 1666; united to
St Lawrence Jewry, 1670; united to St Michael Bassishaw, 1897)
OR C 1558-1677, M 1559-1666, B 1558-1665 (receipts for B 1518-1606) (C 1677+, MB 1670+
at St Lawrence Jewry) (GL)
BT 1639-40 (GL)
Cop C 1558-1666, M 1559-1666, B 1558-1665 (Ptd, HS 72, 1942); C 1666-77 (Ptd, HS 70,
1940); C 1558-1666, M 1559-1666 (IGI); M 1559-1666 (Boyd)

ST MARY MAGDALENE, OLD FISH STREET (762) (united to St Gregory by St Paul's, 1670;
closed and united to St Martin Ludgate, 1890)
OR C 1539-1645, 1665-1892, M 1539-1639, 1665-1886, Banns 1755-70, 1790-1958,
B 1539-1643, 1665-1853 (the 1539-1645 register was, for many years, deposited as part of a
court case, and its location unknown; C 1892+, M 1886+ at St Martin Ludgate) (GL);
ML 1687-1834 (C of A)
BT 1800-21 (GL)
Cop M 1539-1639, 1754-1837, Banns 1755-70 (Ts GL, SG, CRW); M 1664-1754
(GL: Challen 10, SG); C 1539-1645, 1664-1875, M 1538-1877 (IGI); M 1664-1754 (Boyd);
M 1800-37 (Pallot Index); B 1813-53 (CLBI)

ST MARY MOUNTHAW, Old Fish Street Hill (374) (destroyed 1666; united to
St Mary Somerset, 1670; united to St Nicholas Cole Abbey and St Nicholas Olave, 1866)
OR C 1568-1887, M 1568-1666, 1754-1809, 1814-35, 1837-49, B 1568-1849 (C 1887+,
M 1671-1754, 1849+ at St Mary Somerset) (GL)
BT 1800-04, 1807-19 (no M 1802, 1810-13) (GL)
Cop C 1568-1837, M 1568-1835, B 1568-1849 (Ptd, HS 58, 1928); C 1838-40 (Ts I GL, SG,
CRW); C 1568-1837, 1849-75, M 1568-1666, 1754-1835, 1837-49 (IGI); M 1568-1666,
1754-75, 1801-35 (Boyd); M 1780-1837 (Pallot Index); B 1813-49 (CLBI)

ST MARY SOMERSET, Upper Thames Street (221) (united to St Mary Mounthaw, 1670;
united to St Nicholas Cole Abbey, 1866; demolished apart from tower, 1871)
OR C 1559-1880, M 1559-1709, 1711-1878, Banns 1754-58, B 1558-1853 (C 1880+, M 1878+
at St Nicholas Cole Abbey) (GL)
BT 1800-05, 1807-29, 1831-32 (GL)
Cop CM 1559-1837 (Ptd, HS 59, 1929); B 1558-1853 (Ptd, HS 60, 1930); C 1838-40
(Ts I GL, SG, CRW); C 1559-1871, M 1559-1878 (IGI); M 1559-75, 1801-37 (Boyd);
M 1780-1837 (Pallot Index); B 1813-53 (CLBI)

ST MARY STAINING, Staining Lane (309) (destroyed 1666; united to St Michael Wood Street,
1670; united to St Alban Wood Street, 1894; united to St Vedast, Foster Lane, 1954)
OR C 1673-1812 (receipts for B 1644-78, 1707-18, 1749-1836) (all other registers destroyed
by enemy action in 1940) (GL)
BT 1629-31, 1800-03, 1805-20 (GL)
Cop C 1629-31, 1673-1812, M 1629-31, B 1629-31, 1805, 1807-12 (Ts I GL, SG, CRW);
C 1673-1812 (IGI)

ST MARY STAINING Haberdashers' Hall, Staining Lane (Independent)
OR C 1785-1825 (PRO: RG 4/4243); C 1832-38 (GL)
Cop C 1785-1825 (IGI)

ST MARY WOOLCHURCH HAW, Poultry and Cornhill (247) (destroyed 1666; united to
St Mary Woolnoth, 1670)
OR C 1558-1889, M 1559-1666, 1670-1837, Banns 1754-1865, B 1558-1666, 1670-1848
(C 1889+, M 1837+, Banns 1865+ at St Mary Woolnoth) (GL)
BT 1629-31, 1639-40, 1801-30 (GL)
Cop C 1558-1694, 1699, M 1559-1666, B 1558-1666 (Ptd, Brooke and Hallen, 1886);
C 1813-89, M 1814-37, B 1813-48 (Ts I GL, SG, CRW); C 1558-1699, M 1559-1666 (IGI);
M 1559-1666 (Boyd); M 1800-37 (Pallot Index); B 1813-48 (CLBI)

ST MARY WOOLNOTH, Lombard Street (414) (united to St Mary Woolchurch Haw, 1670)
OR C 1538-1985, M 1538-1715, 1727-32, 1744-1953, Banns 1754-67, 1782-1951,
B 1538-1722, 1744-1852 (receipts for B 1722-44, coffins 1726-44) (GL)
BT 1629-30, 1639-40, 1665-66, 1801-30, 1840-42 (no C 1840, M 1840-42) (GL)
Cop C 1538-1760, M 1538-1715, 1727-32, 1745-54, B 1538-1722, 1744-60 (Ptd, Brooke and
Hallen, 1886); C 1761-1840, M 1754-1837, B 1761-1852 (Ts I GL, SG, CRW);
C 1538-1830, M 1538-1885 (IGI); M 1538-1754 (Boyd); M 1800-37 (Pallot Index);
B 1813-52 (CLBI)

ST MATTHEW, Friday Street (225) (united to St Peter Westcheap, 1670; closed 1882;
united to St Vedast, Foster Lane, 1882)
OR C 1813-82 (incomplete), M 1814-36, B 1813-46 (CMB 1538-1812 destroyed by enemy
action, 1940) (GL); M 1837-89 (duplicate at London City Register Office, Finsbury)
(C 1882+, M 1889+ at St Vedast, but destroyed by enemy action, 1940)
BT 1665-66, 1800-Apr 1802, May 1803-May 1804, Dec 1805-Jan 1809, Dec 1809-Dec 1811,
1813-44, 1848-55 (no M 1813, 1837-55, no B 1845-55) (GL)
Cop CMB 1538-1812 (Ptd, HS 63, 1933); M 1538-1836 (GL: Challen 12); C 1813-40, B 1813-46
(Ts I GL, SG, CRW); C 1538-1875, M 1538-1836 (IGI); M 1538-1775, 1801-36 (Boyd);
M 1780-1837 (Pallot Index); B 1813-46 (CLBI)

ST MICHAEL BASSISHAW, Basinghall Street (661) (closed 1892; united to St Lawrence Jewry,
1897)
OR C 1538-1892, M 1538-1665, 1672-1890, Banns 1755-1892, ML 1841-90, B 1538-1853 (GL)
BT 1629-31, 1800-03, 1807-22, 1834-45, 1847-48 (no Jun-Dec 1822, no M Jan-May 1822,
1837-48, no B Jan-May 1822) (GL)
Cop M 1764-1837 (GL)
CMB 1538-1625 (Ptd, HS 72, 1942); C 1626-1733, M 1626-1733, B 1626-1735 (Ptd, HS 73,
1943); C 1733-1892, M 1733-1837, B 1735-1853 (Ptd, HS 74, 1944); C 1538-1875,
M 1538-1880 (IGI); M 1538-1764 (Boyd); M 1764-1837 (Pallot Index); B 1813-53 (CLBI)

ST MICHAEL CORNHILL (508) (united to St Peter le Poer and St Benet Fink, 1906)
OR 1546-1986, M 1546-1836, Banns 1653-60, 1754-87, 1853-1931, B 1546-1853 (receipts for B
1455-1475, 1547-59) (GL); M 1837+ (Inc)
BT 1629-31, 1800-04, 1806-60, 1862-63, 1865-87 (no M 1837-87, no B 1854-87) (GL)
Cop B 1455-1475, 1547-59 (from B receipts, Ptd, Overall, 1871); CMB 1546-1754 (Ptd, HS 7,
1882); C 1754-1840, M 1754-1837, B 1754-1853 (Ts I GL, SG, CRW); C 1545-1754,
1783-1812, M 1546-1836 (IGI); M 1546-1650, 1701-75, 1801-36 (Boyd); M 1800-37 (Pallot
Index); B 1813-53 (CLBI)

ST MICHAEL CROOKED LANE (327) (closed and united to St Magnus the Martyr, 1831)
OR C 1539-1890, M 1539-1835, Banns 1779-1952, ML 1754-1830, B 1538-1852 (C 1890+,
M 1837+ at St Magnus the Martyr) (GL)
BT 1802, 1804-07, 1809-12 (LPL); 1813-42, 1844, 1846-48, 1850 (no M 1836-50, no B 1847,
1850) (GL)
Cop C 1538-1890, M 1600-1835, B 1600-1852 (Ms I only GL); M 1539-1779, Banns 1754-79
(GL: Challen 7), M 1779-1835 (GL: Challen 22); C 1749-1875, M 1749-1835 (IGI);
M 1539-1775, 1801-35 (Boyd); M:1780-1835 (Pallot Index); B 1813-52 (CLBI)

ST MICHAEL CROOKED LANE Miles Lane, Cannon Street (Presbyterian)
OR ZC 1786-1825 (PRO: RG 4/4199, 4405)
Cop C 1786-1825 (IGI)

ST MICHAEL LE QUERNE, Cheapside (248) (destroyed 1666; united to St Vedast, Foster
  Lane, 1670; united to St Matthew Friday Street and St Peter Westcheap, 1882)
OR C 1813-84, M 1813-36, B 1813-49 (receipts for B 1514-1726) (C 1686-1812, M 1686-1705,
  1837-c1882, B 1686-1812 destroyed or damaged beyond repair by enemy action, 1940;
  C 1884-96, M 1754-1812 at St Vedast) (GL)
BT 1629-31, 1639-40, 1665-66, Jul 1803-Mar 1806, 1807-57 (no M 1837-57, no B 1850-57)
  (GL)
Cop C 1685-1836 (Ptd, HS 29, 1902); M 1686-1705, 1813-36, B 1686-1837 (Ptd, HS 30, 1903);
  C 1629-31, 1639-40, 1665-66, 1838-40, M 1629-31, 1639-40, 1665-66, B 1629-31, 1639-40,
  1665-66, 1838-49 (Ts GL, SG, CRW); C 1686-1877 (IGI); M 1686-1705, 1813-36 (Boyd);
  M 1800-37 (Pallot Index); B 1813-49 (CLBI)

ST MICHAEL, PATERNOSTER ROYAL, College Street (198) (Peculiar of the Deanery of the
  Arches) (united to St Martin Vintry, 1670; united to All Hallows the Great and All Hallows
  the Less, 1893)
OR C 1558-1975, M 1558-1666, 1695-1954, Banns 1754-1950, ML 1809-1909, 1913-36,
  B 1558-1850 (M 1675-1701 at St Martin Vintry) (GL)
BT 1799, 1801-04, 1811-12 (LPL); 1813-76 (no M 1837-54, no B 1851-54) (GL)
Cop C 1558-1812, M 1558-1837, B 1558-1850 (SG); M 1558-1837 (Ts GL); M 1558-1754
  (GL: Challen 9); C 1813-37 (Ts I GL, SG, CRW); C 1558-1854, M 1558-1885 (IGI);
  M 1558-1775, 1801-37 (Boyd); M 1780-1837 (Pallot Index); B 1813-50 (CLBI)

ST MICHAEL QUEENHITHE, Upper Thames Street (773) (united to Holy Trinity the Less,
  1670; united to St James Garlickhithe, 1875)
OR C 1653-1876, M 1653-1875, Banns 1754-1812, 1823-75, ML 1731-32, B 1653-1852 (receipts
  for B 1624-25, 1672-84, 1690-97; C 1876+, M 1875+ at St James Garlickhithe) (GL)
BT 1639-40, 1665-66, 1800, Mar 1801-Apr 1803, Jul 1803-May 1805, 1807-60, 1862-75,
  1877-80 (no M 1837-80, no B 1853-80) (GL)
Cop M 1653-1753 (GL: Challen 27); M 1639-40, 1754-1837, Banns 1754-1812 (Ts I GL, SG,
  CRW); C 1653-1875, M 1653-1711 (IGI); M 1701-53 (Boyd); M 1780-1837 (Pallot Index);
  B 1800-13 (Ts SG); B 1813-52 (CLBI)

ST MICHAEL WOOD STREET (404) (united to St Mary Staining, 1670; united to St Alban,
  Wood Street, 1894; united to St Vedast, Foster Lane, 1954)
OR C 1559-1663, M 1559-1661, 1754-1812, Banns 1754-1815, B 1559-1660, 1678-1812
  (receipts for B 1619-1718) (C 1663-c1895, M 1674-1754, 1813-95, B 1813-c1853 destroyed
  by enemy action, 1940, but see coverage of marriages in Boyd and Pallot indexes) (GL);
  M 1838-95 (duplicate at London City Register Office, Finsbury Town Hall)
BT 1629-30, 1639-40, 1800-11, 1813-20 (GL)
Cop C 1559-1662, 1800-11, 1813-20, M 1559-1661, 1754-1820, Banns 1754-1815, B 1559-1660,
  1678-1811, 1813-20 (Ts GL, SG, CRW); C 1559-1662, 1801-11, M 1801-11 (IGI);
  M 1674-1837 (Boyd); M 1800-37 (Pallot Index); B 1813-20 (CLBI)

ST MILDRED BREAD STREET (302) (united to St Margaret Moses, 1670; destroyed 1941;
  united to St Mary le Bow, 1954)
OR M 1754-1837, Banns 1754-74, B 1813-53 (receipts for B 1648-67, 1741-1806) (C 1659-1941,
  M 1671-1754, 1837-1941, B 1670-1812 destroyed by enemy action, 1941) (GL)
BT 1629-31, 1639-40, 1800-29, 1832-42 (no M 1828-29) (GL)
Cop C 1659-1837, M 1670-1837, Banns 1754-74, B 1670-1853 (Ptd, HS 42, 1912);
  CMB 1629-31, 1639-40, C 1838-1842 (Ts I GL, SG, CRW); C 1658-1837, M 1670-1837
  (IGI); M 1670-1837 (Boyd); M 1780-1837 (Pallot Index); B 1813-53 (CLBI)

ST MILDRED POULTRY (285) (united to St Mary Colechurch, 1670; closed and united to
St Olave Jewry, 1871; united to St Margaret Lothbury, 1886)
OR C 1538-1870, M 1538-1871, Banns 1756-65, 1792-1865, 1870, ML 1810-70, B 1538-1852
(C 1870+, M 1871+ at St Olave Jewry) (GL)
BT 1800, 1802-03, 1807-11, 1813-33 (GL)
Cop M 1538-1754 (GL: Challen 8); M 1754-1837, Banns 1756-65 (Ts I GL, SG, CRW);
C 1538-1870, M 1538-1837 (IGI); M 1538-1754 (Boyd); M 1800-03, 1807-37 (Pallot Index);
B 1813-52 (CLBI)

ST MILDRED POULTRY Poultry Chapel (Independent) (f early 18th century in Camomile
Street, All Hallows, the Poultry Chapel was built on the site of the old Poultry Compter, in
St Mildred Poultry parish, 1819; it was renamed the City Temple, 1872)
OR C 1702-53, 1781-1837 (PRO: RG 4/4207, 4410) (registers 1837-c1940 destroyed by enemy
action, 1940)
Cop C 1702-1837 (IGI)

ST NICHOLAS ACONS, Nicholas Lane (228) (destroyed 1666; united to St Edmund the King
and Martyr, 1670)
OR C 1540-1875, M 1539-1664, 1813-49, B 1540-1848 (C 1875+, M 1673-1812, 1849+,
Banns 1811+ at St Edmund the King and Martyr) (GL)
BT 1629-31, 1639-40, 1800-03, 1807-60 (no M 1807, 1838-60, no B 1849-60) (GL)
Cop C 1540-1812, M 1539-1664, B 1540-1812 (Ptd, W. Brigg, 1890); C 1813-41, M 1813-37,
B 1813-48 (Ts I GL, SG, CRW); C 1539-1875, M 1539-1664, 1813-37 (IGI); M 1539-1664
(Boyd); M 1780-1837 (Pallot Index); B 1813-48 (CLBI)

ST NICHOLAS COLE ABBEY, Knightrider Street, Queen Victoria Street (209) (united to
St Nicholas Olave, 1670; united to St Mary Somerset and St Mary Mounthaw, 1866; united
to St Benet Paul's Wharf and St Peter Paul's Wharf, 1879)
OR C 1539-1975, Z 1698-1701, M 1584-1753, 1755-1946, Banns 1754-1889, B 1538-1647,
1651-1851 (GL)
BT 1639-40, 1665-66, 1800-02, Mar 1803-Mar 1804, 1807-08, Aug 1809-31, 1833-45
(no M 1838-45) (GL)
Cop C 1538-1812, M 1584-1812, B 1538-1812 (SG); M 1813-37, 1873 (Ts I GL, SG, CRW);
C 1538-1875, M 1584-1885 (IGI); M 1584-1812 (Boyd); M 1800-37 (Pallot Index);
B 1813-51 (CLBI)

ST NICHOLAS FLESH SHAMBLES *see* **ST NICHOLAS SHAMBLES**

ST NICHOLAS OLAVE, Bread Street Hill (372) (destroyed 1666; united to St Nicholas Cole
Abbey, 1670; united to St Mary Somerset and St Mary Mounthaw, 1866; united to St Benet
Paul's Wharf and St Peter Paul's Wharf, 1879)
OR C 1704-1908, 1936, M 1705-20, 1813-36, B 1704-1852 (C 1670-1704, 1908+,
M 1670-1704, 1721-1812, 1837+, Banns 1754-1889, B 1670-1704 at St Nicholas Cole
Abbey) (GL)
BT 1800-03, 1807-45 (no C 1809, no M 1811, 1832, 1837-45, no B 1809) (GL)
Cop C 1704-1840, M 1705-20, 1813-36, B 1704-1852 (Ts I GL, SG, CRW); C 1704-1875,
M 1705-20, 1813-36 (IGI); B 1813-52 (CLBI)

ST NICHOLAS SHAMBLES (destroyed at Dissolution; incorporated with St Audoen in
Christ Church Greyfriars, 1547)
OR CMB 1538-47 (CMB 1547+ at Christ Church) (GL)

ST OLAVE HART STREET (1,041) (united to All Hallows Staining, 1870; united to
St Katherine Coleman, 1921)
OR C 1563-1978, M 1563-1961, Banns 1754-1815, 1823-26, 1840-1936, B 1563-1853, Interment
of ashes 1959-64 (GL)
BT 1629-30, 1665-66, 1802-46 (no C 1812, no M 1836-46) (GL)
Cop CMB 1563-1701 (Ptd, HS 46, 1916); M 1701-54 (GL: Challen 12); C 1563-1878,
M 1563-1876 (IGI); M 1563-1754 (Boyd); M 1780-1837 (Pallot Index); B 1813-53 (CLBI 3)

ST OLAVE OLD JEWRY (213) (demolished 1887; united to St Martin Pomeroy, 1670; united to
St Margaret Lothbury, 1886)
OR C 1539-1884, M 1539-1886, Banns 1771-1803, 1824-50, 1852-86, B 1538-1849 (C 1884+,
M 1886+, Banns 1886+ at St Margaret Lothbury) (GL)
BT 1629-31, 1800-01, Mar 1802-03, 1807-18, 1832-37, 1854-56, 1858 (no MB 1854-58) (GL)
Cop M 1538-1754 (GL: Challen 8, SG); M 1754-1837 (Ts I GL, SG, CRW); C 1538-1875,
M 1538-1885 (IGI); M 1538-1754 (Boyd); M 1800-37 (Pallot Index); B 1813-49 (CLBI)

ST OLAVE OLD JEWRY Presbyterian Church, Meeting House Court
OR C 1716-1819, B 1786-87 (PRO: RG 4/4349, 4408)
Cop C 1716-1819 (IGI)

ST OLAVE SILVER STREET (711) (destroyed 1666; united to St Alban, Wood Street, 1670;
united to St Vedast, Foster Lane, 1954)
OR C 1562-1770, M 1562-1680, 1743, B 1561-1770 (receipts for B 1757-93) (C 1770-1812,
B 1770-1812 destroyed or damaged beyond repair by enemy action, 1940; CB 1813+,
M 1681+ at St Alban Wood Street) (GL)
BT 1639-40, 1665-66, 1800-05, 1807-12 (GL)
Cop C Oct 1770-Nov 1772, Oct 1773-Sep 1774 (Ms I GL); C 1562-1774, 1800-05, 1807-12,
M 1562-1680, 1800-05, 1807-12, B 1561-1770, 1800-05, 1807-12 (Ts CRW, GL, SG);
C 1616-1736 (IGI); M 1800-37 (Pallot Index)

ST OLAVE SILVER STREET Lamb's Chapel alias **ST JAMES IN THE WALL**,
Monkwell Street (demolished, 1872)
OR C 1621-27, M 1619-26, 1640, 1688, 1696-98, 1709-53 (GL)
Cop C 1621-27, M 1619-26, 1640, 1688, 1696-98, 1709-53 (Ts I GL, SG, CRW)

ST PANCRAS SOPER LANE, Pancras Lane (168) (destroyed 1666; united to St Mary le Bow,
1670)
OR C 1538-1698, 1813-89, M 1538-1674, 1818-36, B 1538-1697, 1813-49 (C 1698-1812,
1889+, M 1675-1812, Banns 1754-1937, B 1698-1812 at St Mary le Bow) (GL)
BT 1817-46, 1848-58 (no M 1817, 1837-58, no B 1850-58) (GL)
Cop C 1538-1837, B 1538-1852 (Ptd, HS 44, 1914); M 1538-1837 (Ptd, HS 45, 1915);
C 1838-40 (Ts I GL, SG, CRW); C 1538-1875, M 1538-1674, 1818-36 (IGI); M 1538-1674,
1818-37 (Boyd); M 1780-1837 (Pallot Index); B 1813-49 (CLBI)

ST PAUL'S CATHEDRAL (non-parochial) (destroyed 1666; rebuilt 1675-1710)
OR M 1697-1740, ML 1877-1980, B 1706, 1735, 1760-1812 (receipts for B 1525-26, 1535-36,
1548-50, 1554-57, 1570-84, 1592-94; some B 1559-1626 at St Gregory by St Paul's) (GL);
C 1708-13, 1875-1975, M 1740-58, 1877-1982, B 1814+ (The Cathedral)
BT 1814-20, 1825-38 (no CM 1814-38) (GL)
Cop C 1708-13, 1875-97, M 1697-1758, 1877-96, B 1760-1899 (Ptd, HS 26, 1898);
M 1697-1758 (Boyd); C 1708-13, 1875-1939, M 1697-1758, 1877-1939, B 1760-1936 (Ms I
only GL); B 1813-53 (CLBI 3)

ST PETER CORNHILL (729)
OR C 1538-1951, M 1539-1985, Banns 1754-1977, B 1539-1853 (GL)
BT 1639-40, 1800, Apr 1801-Apr 1804, 1808-60, 1862-93 (no M 1892-93, no B 1854-93) (GL)
Cop C 1538-1666, MB 1539-1666 (Ptd, HS 1, 1877); CB 1667-1774, M 1673-1754 (Ptd, HS 4,
1879); C 1775-1840, M 1754-1837, B 1775-1853 (Ts I GL, SG, CRW); C 1538-1875,
M 1538-1837 (IGI); M 1538-1754 (Boyd); M 1780-1837 (Pallot Index); B 1813-53 (CLBI)

ST PETER LE POER, Old Broad Street (546) (united to St Benet Fink, 1842; closed 1905; united
to St Michael Cornhill, 1906)
OR C 1561-1905, M 1561-1904, Banns 1653-55, 1755-1817, B 1561-1853 (C 1905+, M 1904+
at St Michael Cornhill) (GL)
BT 1809-30, 1832-33, 1838-41, 1845-90 (no M 1838-90, no B 1854-90) (GL)
Cop M 1561-1837 (GL: Challen 7, SG); C 1561-1905, M 1561-1904, B 1561-1853 (Ts GL);
C 1561-1875, M 1561-1722 (IGI); M 1561-1775, 1801-37 (Boyd); M 1780-1837 (Pallot
Index); B 1813-53 (CLBI 3)

ST PETER LE POER Pinners' Hall, Broad Street (Independent)
OR C 1740-1824 (PRO: RG 4/4134-35, 4226)
Cop C 1740-1824 (IGI)

ST PETER LE POER Dutch Church, Austin Friars
OR C 1559-61, 1563-67, 1570-1874, M 1559-61, 1563, 1571-1752, 1812, 1857-71,
　　Proclamations of M 1643-1752, B 1559-61, 1671-1853 (GL)
Cop C 1559-61, 1563-67, M 1559-61, 1563, B 1559-61 (Ptd, A.A. Van Schelven, 1923);
　　C 1570-1874, M 1571-1752, 1812, 1857-71, B 1671-1853 (Ptd, W.J.C. Moens, 1884);
　　M 1571-1812 (Boyd); B 1813-53 (CLBI 3)

ST PETER, PAUL'S WHARF, Thames Street (354) (destroyed 1666; united to St Benet Paul's
　　Wharf, 1670; united to St Nicholas Cole Abbey, 1879)
OR C 1607-1886, M 1607-49, 1653-60, 1684, B 1607-1849 (C 1886+, M 1680+ at St Benet
　　Paul's Wharf) (GL)
BT 1800-51, 1854-65, 1867-72 (no M 1800-01, 1803-04, 1809, 1812-72, no B 1850-72) (GL)
Cop C 1607-1837 (Ptd, HS 38, 1909); M 1607-60, 1684, 1698-1705, 1828-34 (Ptd, HS 40,
　　1911); B 1607-1837 (Ptd, HS 41, 1912); B 1838-49 (Ts I GL, SG, CRW); C 1607-1837,
　　M 1607-25, 1639-60, 1698-1704, 1828-34 (IGI); M 1607-60, 1684, 1698-1705, 1828-34
　　(Boyd); M 1780-1837 (Pallot Index); B 1813-49 (CLBI)

ST PETER WESTCHEAP, Wood Street (226) (destroyed 1666; united to St Matthew,
　　Friday Street, 1670; united to St Vedast, Foster Lane, 1882)
OR C 1538-98, 1813-76, M 1538-98, 1814-36, B 1538-98, 1813-46 (receipts for B 1534-1671,
　　1681-99, 1702-21, 1730-32, 1739-54, 1762-63) (C 1599-1810, M 1599-1699, B 1599-1812
　　destroyed by enemy action, 1940; M 1699-1812 at St Matthew Friday Street, registers
　　destroyed, 1940, but transcripts available) (GL)
BT 1629-31, 1800-Apr 1802, 1807-11, 1813-44, 1848-55 (GL)
Cop M 1754-1812 (Ptd, HS 63, 1933); M 1538-1698, 1814-36 (GL: Challen 12);
　　CB 1538-98, 1629-31, C 1813-40, B 1813-46 (Ts I GL, SG, CRW); C 1538-98, 1813-68,
　　M 1538-98, 1814-36 (IGI); M 1538-1699, 1814-36 (Boyd); M 1780-1837 (Pallot Index);
　　B 1813-46 (CLBI); Extr CB 1538-1812 (C of A: Chester Ms 48); Extr C 1554-1797,
　　B 1542-1791 (GL)

ST SEPULCHRE (alias St Sepulchre without Newgate), Holborn Viaduct (12,479) (united to
　　Christ Church Greyfriars and St Leonard Foster Lane, 1954)
OR C 1662-1886, M 1662-1901, B 1662-1857, Funerals 1900-04 (GL)
BT 1800-60, 1862-91 (no M 1862-91, no B 1858-91) (GL)
Cop C 1663-1714, M 1662-1761, B 1662-1723 (SG); M 1662-1754 (GL: Challen 14);
　　B 1813-57, 1900-04 (Ts I GL, SG, CRW); C 1662-1875 (IGI); M 1662-1754 (Boyd);
　　M 1800-37 (Pallot Index); B 1813-57 (CLBI)

ST SEPULCHRE Old Red Hand and Mitre Chapel (one of the places in the Fleet Prison vicinity
　　where clandestine marriages took place)
OR C 1751-53, M 1750-54 (PRO: RG 7/256)
Cop C 1751-53, M 1750-54 (GL: Challen 12, SG)

ST STEPHEN, COLEMAN STREET (4,014) (bombed 1940; united to St Margaret Lothbury,
　　1954)
OR C 1538-1951, M 1538-1952, Banns 1754-1847, ML 1813-1910, B 1538-1853 (receipts for
　　B 1486-1507) (GL)
BT 1800-02, 1807-11, 1813-46, 1849-60, 1862-69 (no M 1838-69, no B 1850-69) (GL)
Cop M 1538-1754 (GL: Challen 25, SG); C 1538-1875, M 1538-1754 (IGI); M 1701-54 (Boyd);
　　M 1780-1837 (Pallot Index); B 1813-53 (CLBI 3)

ST STEPHEN, COLEMAN STREET St Mary Moorfields, Eldon Street (Roman Catholic) f 1710
OR C 1763-1907, M 1763-1821, 1837-67, B 1819-53, 1857-60 (M 1821-37 destroyed by fire)
　　(Westminster Diocesan Archives); C 1907+, M 1867+ (Inc)
Cop C 1763-1834, M 1763-1856, B 1819-53 (Catholic FHS); M 1837-70 (I Institute of Heraldic
　　& Genealogical Studies, Canterbury)

ST STEPHEN, COLEMAN STREET Fletchers' or Finsbury Chapel, Finsbury Circus
(Independent) (from 1824-26 in St Giles Cripplegate, from 1826 to 1889 in St Stephen)
OR C 1824-89, M 1838-64 (GLRO: N/C/6)

ST STEPHEN, COLEMAN STREET Our Saviour (Greek Orthodox) (moved to London Wall,
1849; became the Church of San Sophia, Moscow Road, Bayswater, 1879)
OR CMD 1837+ (Inc)

ST STEPHEN WALBROOK (281) (united to St Benet Sherehog, 1670; united to St Swithin
London Stone, 1954)
OR C 1557-1946, M 1557-1940, Banns 1754-1954, B 1557-1860 (receipts for B 1474-1538,
1548-1637) (GL); C 1946+, M 1940+ (Inc)
BT 1665-66, 1800-03, 1806-37 (GL)
Cop C 1557-1790, M 1557-1754, B 1557-1716 (Ptd, HS 49, 1919); C 1790-1860, M 1754-1860,
Banns 1754-1841, B 1716-1860 (Ptd, HS 50, 1920); C 1557-1877, M 1557-1880 (IGI);
M 1557-1837 (Boyd); M 1780-1860 (Pallot Index); B 1813-60 (CLBI)

ST SWITHIN LONDON STONE, Cannon Street (486) (united to St Mary Bothaw, 1670;
bombed 1940; united to St Stephen, Walbrook and St Benet Sherehog, 1954)
OR C 1615-1944, M 1619-65, 1672-1941, Banns 1754-60, B 1614-1853, 1935 (GL)
BT 1629-31, 1639-40, 1800-34, 1836-50, 1852-75, 1881-84 (no M 1882-84, no B 1854-84) (GL)
Cop M 1619-65, 1672-1837 (GL: Challen 31); C 1675-1840, B 1666-1853 (Ts I GL, SG, CRW);
C 1615-1875 (IGI); M 1726-75, 1801-37 (Boyd); M 1780-1837 (Pallot Index); B 1813-53
(CLBI)
Cop (Mf) C 1615-75, M 1619-65, B 1614-65 (SG)

ST THOMAS THE APOSTLE, Great St Thomas Apostle (531) (destroyed 1666; united to
St Mary Aldermary, 1670; united to St Antholin and St John the Baptist on Walbrook, 1873)
OR C 1558-1680, 1704-1873, M 1558-1672, 1754-1869, Banns 1754-68, 1770-1873,
B 1558-1680, 1754-1849 (C 1873+, M 1672-1754, 1869+, Banns 1873+ at St Mary
Aldermary) (GL)
BT 1639-40, 1800-49 (no M 1811-12, 1836-49) (GL)
Cop C 1558-1680, 1704-54, M 1558-1672, B 1558-1680, 1704-54 (Ptd, HS 6, 1881);
C 1754-1840, M 1754-1837, B 1754-1849 (Ts I GL, SG, CRW); C 1558-1873,
M 1558-1672, 1754-1835 (IGI); M 1558-1672; M 1800-37 (Pallot Index); B 1813-49 (CLBI)

ST THOMAS THE APOSTLE St Boniface (German Church), Great St Thomas Apostle, Bow
Lane until 1859, now Adler Street, Commercial Road (Roman Catholic) f 1809 (Cath Dir
1965)
OR C 1809+, M 1864+, D 1876+ (Inc)
Cop C 1809-1950, M 1864-1968 (Anglo-German FHS)

ST VEDAST, Foster Lane (496) (Peculiar of the Deanery of the Arches) (united to St Michael le
Querne, 1670; united to St Matthew Friday Street and St Peter Westcheap, 1882; united to
St Alban Wood Street, St Olave Silver Street, St Michael Wood Street, St Mary Staining,
St Anne and St Agnes and St John Zachary, 1954)
OR M 1754-1837, 1954-81, Banns 1754-1809, B 1813-53 (C 1558-1940, Z 1695-1705,
M 1559-1754, 1838-c1940, 1558-1812 destroyed or damaged beyond repair by enemy action,
1940) (GL); C c1940+ (Inc)
BT 1799-1800, 1803-08, 1810-12 (LPL); 1813-59 (no M 1859, no B 1852-59) (GL)
Cop C 1558-1836, Z 1695-1705 (Ptd, HS 29, 1902); M 1559-1837, B 1558-1837 (Ptd, HS 30,
1903); C 1837-1840, B 1838-53 (Ts GL, SG, CRW); C 1558-1836, M 1558-1837 (IGI);
M 1559-1837 (Boyd); M 1780-1837 (Pallot Index); B 1813-53 (CLBI)

TEMPLE CHURCH St Mary the Virgin
OR C 1629+, M 1628-1760, B 1629-1853 (The Master, Temple, London, EC4)
Cop C 1629-1853, M 1628-1760 (Ptd, HS NS 1, 1979; B 1629-1852 (Ptd, H.G. Woods, 1905);
B 1813-53 (CLBI)

TOWER OF LONDON *see* **ST PETER ad VINCULA** in Middlesex section

WHITECHAPEL St Mary (six houses were in the City of London to 1900, when this part of the parish was transferred to St Botolph Aldgate; *see* Middlesex section)

WHITEFRIARS PRECINCT (1,302) (an extra-parochial area, consisting of the precinct or liberty of the site of the former house of Carmelite or White Friars on the south side of Fleet Street between Bridewell and the Temple) (inhabitants used St Bride and St Dunstan until 1842 when Holy Trinity Gough Square was formed)

MIDDLESEX

General information   39
Record offices and libraries   39
Ecclesiastical divisions and original parish registers   39
Bishop's transcripts   41
Modern copies of parish registers
Printed   41
Typescript and manuscript   41
Microform   42
Marriage indexes   42
Allegations for marriage licences   42
Cemeteries   43
Nonconformist records   43
 Jews   43
 Roman Catholics   44
 Independents and Congregationalists   44
 Baptists   44
 Methodists   44
 Presbyterians   44
 Irvingites   45
 Swedenborgians   45
 Society of Friends (Quakers)   45
 Foreign churches   47
Newspapers   47
Bibliography   47
Abbreviations   48
Parish listings   **49**

MIDDLESEX

GENERAL INFORMATION

The ancient county of Middlesex has disappeared in all but name, absorbed by the relentless growth of London itself. In 1888, 31,484 acres were taken from it to help form the new County of London. At the same time 771 acres were transferred to Hertfordshire. In 1965 the remaining 149,668 acres were split, by far the greater part becoming part of the new Greater London area, but a few parishes in the extreme south-west being transferred to the administrative county of Surrey. The ancient county's borders were mainly natural features. The River Thames divided it from Surrey and Kent in the south, the River Lea from Essex in the east, and the River Colne from Buckinghamshire in the west. Only in the north did it have an arbitrary (and irregular) boundary from Hertfordshire.

It is a small county (only Rutland is smaller among the ancient English counties) but of much greater importance than its geographical size due to the proximity of London and the institutions, commerce and industry associated with the capital.

RECORD OFFICES AND LIBRARIES

London Metropolitan Archives, 40 Northampton Road, London EC1R 0HB. 9.30 am to 7.30 pm Tuesday (advance booking necessary for original documents), 9.30 am to 4.45 Wednesday to Friday. The office is also open some Saturdays. It is necessary to check dates in advance of a visit. (Tel: 020-7606-3030)
This office holds the vast majority of London and Middlesex parish records, outside the Cities of London and Westminster.

Guildhall Library, Aldermanbury, London EC2P 2EJ. 9.30 am to 4.45 pm Monday to Saturday (Tel: 020-7260-1683).
This library, in addition to City of London records, holds the registers of the Middlesex parishes of Shoreditch and St Katharine by the Tower.

City of Westminster Archives Centre, 10 St Ann's Street, London SW1P 2XR. 9.30 am to 7 pm Monday to Friday, 9.30 am to 5 pm Saturday. (Tel: 020-7798-2180).
This holds most of the registers of parishes within the City of Westminster, apart from St Margaret.

Hammersmith and Fulham Archives and Local History Centre, The Lilla Huset, 191 Talgarth Road, London W6 8BJ. 9.30 am to 8 pm Monday, 9.30 am to 1 pm Tuesday, Thursday and first Saturday in the month (advance booking essential for all visits) (Tel: 020-8741-5159).
This holds the registers of St Paul Hammersmith.

Hounslow Library, Local Studies Department, 24 Treaty Centre, High Street, Hounslow TW3 1ES. 9.30 am to 8 pm Tuesday, Thursday, 9.30 to 5.30 Monday, Wednesday, Friday, Saturday (Tel: 020-8570-0622).
This holds the original, damaged, registers of Isleworth. There are film copies at London Metropolitan Archives.

Hertfordshire Archives and Local Studies, County Hall, Pegs Lane, Hertford SG13 8EJ. Monday, Wednesday, Thursday 9.30 am to 5.30 pm, Friday 9.30 am to 4.30 pm, Saturday 9 am to 1 pm. (Tel: 01992-555105).

This holds the records of Potters Bar.

ECCLESIASTICAL DIVISIONS AND ORIGINAL PARISH REGISTERS

Middlesex is and has always been entirely in the diocese of London, apart from Peculiars. The most strange of these is Ely Place, Holborn, which was technically part of Cambridgeshire and the diocese of Ely, as the London home of bishops of Ely.

The Peculiar of the Deanery of Croydon included Harrow, Hayes, Norwood and Pinner. The parishes of Chiswick, West Drayton, Friern Barnet, St Luke Old Street, St Pancras, Stoke Newington and Willesden were in the Peculiar of the Dean and Chapter of St Paul's Cathedral. Paddington, St John Westminster and St Margaret Westminster constituted the Royal Peculiar of the Dean and Chapter of Westminster. St Katharine by the Tower was a single parish Royal Peculiar. There were various other minor special jurisdictions such as the Savoy Chapel.

Middlesex registers have an average starting date of 1595, early, but not startlingly so for a county in the south-east of England, indeed it is exactly the same as its southern neighbour Surrey.

Seven registers begin in 1538 (Harefield, Laleham, St Peter ad Vincula, Staines, Stratford le Bow, Twickenham and Uxbridge), five more in 1539 (Acton, Greenford, Ickenham, Kensington and St Margaret Westminster) and one in 1540 (Harlington). Seven more sequences start before Elizabeth I's accession, eleven in 1558 and three in the next year. Therefore over 40% of Middlesex register series start within a year or two of the beginning of Elizabeth's reign. 19 more series start before 1600, so that 53 (or two-thirds) of Middlesex register series start before the end of the sixteenth century.

Just six sequences start in the 1600-1649 period, but sixteen more start before the end of the seventeenth century. Just five parishes (all small rural places) have registers which do not start until after 1700 (Perivale 1707, Edgware 1717, West Twyford 1722, Hanworth 1731 and Kingsbury 1732).

Because of the growth of London, and despite the low ebb of the Church of England in the eighteenth century, new parishes were founded from the late seventeenth century on, in gradually rising numbers until the explosion of new church building in the 1830s and later.

The first developments were mainly in the west with Covent Garden (1653), St James Westminster (1685), St Anne Soho (1686) and St George the Martyr, Queen Square (1706) though in the east Shadwell had been created in 1670. The first half of the eighteenth century saw Bethnal Green (1746), Bloomsbury (1730), St John Clerkenwell (1723), Stratford le Bow (1719), Limehouse (1725), Wapping (1729), Poplar (1711), St George Hanover Square (1725), St George in the East (1729), St John Westminster (1728), St Luke Old Street (1733, taking the Middlesex part of St Giles Cripplegate) and Spitalfields (1729).

There was then a complete cessation of parish creation until the 1820s, despite the huge growth in population of many suburbs. In some parishes, chapels were established by private efforts. In the 1820s there began a systematic expansion of church provision. Many highly-populated parishes had several new parishes created either simultaneously or over a short period. Thus in St Marylebone, All Souls, Christ Church and St Mary Bryanstone Square were all founded in 1825, and Holy Trinity three years later. Similarly Islington had Holy Trinity founded in 1829 and St John and St Paul founded in the next year. In other parishes, the process was more gradual, but eleven parishes in Middlesex were founded in the 1820s, and no less than 21 in the period 1830-1837. Even quite rural areas such as Hampton and Norwood saw new churches.

For the inner area, the London Metropolitan Archives has been successful in securing the deposit of almost all the older registers. Hampstead, Kensington, the Savoy and St Giles in the Fields have not deposited, but for Kensington there is a full transcript at the Society of Genealogists, and for Hampstead there is a film in Holborn Local Studies Library. For St Giles in the Fields apart from a transcript of the marriages up to 1650, there is no alternative until the bishop's transcripts start in 1800, and for the Savoy there is only a (? complete) transcript to the 1820s at the College of Arms, no more publicly available than the originals. It should also be noted that Shoreditch is deposited at the Guildhall Library, rather than the London Metropolitan Archives and the Westminster parishes are deposited at the City of Westminster Archives Centre.

For the outer area, the London Metropolitan Archives has been somewhat less successful in attracting deposit, though a number of parishes have deposited since the first edition of this book in 1995. The following ancient parishes have still not deposited their registers: Chiswick, Greenford,

Harlington, Shepperton and Twickenham. However, there are substitutes for most: there is a full transcript of Harlington at the Society of Genealogists and the London Metropolitan Archives; Chiswick and Shepperton have full transcripts at the Society of Genealogists only. Twickenham also has a transcript there, but the baptism transcript ends in 1831, the bishop's transcripts need to be used for the later period. The marriages of Greenford have been printed, but there is no other transcript apart from a very imperfect set of bishop's transcripts from 1800. Hammersmith is deposited at Hammersmith and Fulham Archives. Isleworth is deposited at Hounslow Library, but there is a film at London Metropolitan Archives.

BISHOP'S TRANSCRIPTS

The bishop's transcripts of Middlesex are a poor resource. Apart from the rather doubtful case of a Fulham transcript apparently dating from 1614, there are no transcripts before 1629. For the period 1629-31 there survive transcripts for 29 parishes, from the period 1639-1640 for 30 parishes. There are a very few for other scattered years, three parishes having returns in the 1663-1666 period, a 1671 return (and those for 1702-1703) survive for Harrow, 1671-1674 for Norwood, 1745-1756 for Chelsea, 1768 for Isleworth, 1798-1799 for Stratford le Bow, and 1799 for Harrow, Hayes and Pinner.

The main sequence of transcripts only starts in 1800 for the majority of parishes. 27 parishes have *no* earlier transcript at all, and one sequence each starts in 1801, 1802, 1803 and 1805. In 1807 four sequences start (St James Clerkenwell, St John Clerkenwell, St Clement Danes and Shoreditch), one in 1810 (West Twyford) and in 1813 no less than twelve (Chiswick, West Drayton, Friern Barnet, Harefield, Poplar, St John Westminster, St Luke Old Street, St Margaret Westminster, St Pancras, Stoke Newington, Westminster Abbey and Willesden). The Peculiars of the Savoy, St Peter ad Vincula and St Katharine by the Tower have no transcripts at all. Nor do Middlesex transcripts run late. Many end in the 1830s, and few postdate the 1850s.

Now doubt this paucity may be explained, at least in part, by their total neglect by those responsible for their care. In the *Athenaeum* of 5 July 1890 (7th Ser. 11 p.94) "W.C.W." refers to the Bishop of London's transcripts which were stored at that time in St Paul's Cathedral: 'I was once taken to see those transcripts in the dome - some cartloads of them, in a pile, covered with a pall of black dust'. It would seem likely that at some point somebody ordered the destruction of the pre-1800 transcripts; it seems unlikely that they were never made.

MODERN COPIES OF PARISH REGISTERS

PRINTED

A number of Middlesex registers have been printed, the greatest number being of marriages only, in either the Harleian Society register section series, or the Phillimore marriage series. For convenience, these and all City of London printed registers have been listed in the Appendix to the City section of this book.

The Huguenot Society of London has printed all the London registers of its community, and some work has been done on Catholic and Jewish records. Very little has been published of other Nonconformist denominations' registers.

TYPESCRIPT AND MANUSCRIPT

Many Middlesex registers have copies at the Society of Genealogists, and a rather lesser number at the London Metropolitan Archives, and a few at the Guildhall Library. London Metropolitan Archives has a very large collection of unique indexes (as opposed to full copies) to a number of the very highly-populated parishes in its area. They are mainly to baptisms and marriages and concentrate on the period c1770-1837. The indexes were compiled by volunteers, under a programme whereby photocopies were taken of the originals, and an index compiled to each of the registers. This does mean that each parish has a large number of indexes. The Society of Genealogists was recently given many of these indexes; they are available at London Metropolitan

Archives only on microfilm.

MICROFORM

It is now generally regarded as uneconomic to print registers, and certainly is for large urban ones. Most recent work in the field has therefore been produced on microfiche. All of the Middlesex societies have produced microfiche editions of registers and other records, and plan continued programmes of such publications.

As everywhere else, the Genealogical Society of Utah have a large collection of films of Middlesex registers, but their holdings are nothing like as comprehensive outside the City of London as within it. This is reflected, naturally enough, in the coverage of the International Genealogical Index.

MARRIAGE INDEXES

Middlesex is incorporated with the City of London in Boyd's Index. Parts of 58 parishes are included mainly to 1754 or 1812, and several other sources such as the Huguenot churches. Boyd's Index is at the Society of Genealogists, the Guildhall Library has a copy of the London and Middlesex section, and there is a microfilm copy at Salt Lake City.

For the period c1780-1837, the Pallot Index is fairly comprehensive, and especially so after 1800. This index is held by the Institute of Heraldic and Genealogical Studies, 80-82 Northgate, Canterbury, Kent CT1 1BA. This index has been published on CD-Rom by Ancestry.Com. From the CD Rom, one can view the original slip, via the Internet, on Ancestry.Com's website. West Middlesex Marriage Index has some 50,000 entries mainly from West Middlesex up to 1837, and is held by V.E. Gale, 53 Liberty Lane, Addlestone, Weybridge, Surrey KT15 1NQ. The Middlesex Marriage Index 1813-1837 is designed mainly to complement Pallot by covering those parishes not in that index. It is held by the writer (Cold Arbor, Coldharbour Road, Pyrford, Surrey GU22 8SJ) and is currently being digitized for publication, probably on CD Rom. In all of these last three indexes only postal searches are permitted and a fee is charged.

ALLEGATIONS FOR MARRIAGE LICENCES

Various authorities could issue marriage licences to residents of the City of London and Middlesex. The Faculty Office and the Vicar General had wide authority, the former to the whole of England and Wales, the latter to the whole province of Canterbury. Records of both are preserved at Lambeth Palace Library.

The Faculty Office records have been calendared to 1714 (Harleian Society 24, 1886, and British Record Society 33, 1905). However, after 1632 only the names of the parties are given in the latter calendar, while the former publication though it contains some entries to 1869 is gradually less and less comprehensive after 1632. The unprinted calendars are listed chronologically by surname only; there are films of them to 1845 at the Society of Genealogists. The Society of Genealogists has produced name indexes on fiche to the unprinted records. They are also available on the Origins website.

The Vicar General's records only start in 1660. There are printed calendars to the period 1660 to 1694 (Harleian Society 23, 30-31, 33-34, 1886-1892). The Society of Genealogist has typed calendars for the period 1694-1709. The Society of Genealogists has produced name indexes on fiche to the later records. They are also available on the Origins website.

Lambeth Palace Library also holds records for the Peculiar Deanery of the Arches, but these only survive for the period 1686 to 1707, and also for the Peculiar Deanery of Croydon, which survive from 1684 to 1818.

The Bishop of London also had a Vicar General, which causes some confusion. This jurisdiction was over most of London, Middlesex and Essex and parts of Hertfordshire and Buckinghamshire. There is a full printed list of the first period from 1521 to 1597 in Harleian Society 25 (1887). The period 1597-1648 and 1660-1700 are listed in basic form in British Record Society volumes 62 and 66 (1937-1940). Entries which are asterisked in these volumes are included in the selective calendars in Harleian Society 25-26 (1887). Typescript and manuscript calendars of the remainder are with the original records at the Guildhall Library. There is also a typescript index in fourteen volumes at the Society of Genealogists covering the period 1700-45, and the period 1700-75 had slips written for both males and females, and filed in the Great Card Index there.

Also at the Guildhall Library, are records relating to licences issued by the Archdeacon of London (who had jurisdiction over most of the City, Clerkenwell, Islington and Shoreditch) 1666-1691, the Dean and Chapter of St Paul's (who had jurisdiction in his peculiar) 1686-1841 and for the Royal Peculiar of St Katharine by the Tower 1686-1802. Most of the records of this last Peculiar were printed in *Home Counties Magazine* 4-6, 1902-1904.

The Peculiar of the Dean and Chapter of Westminster has records of allegations from 1559. The surviving periods (1559-1646, 1661-1678 and 1688-1699) were printed in Harleian Society 23 (1886). There is also an account book of fees 1772-1804 for this Peculiar at Westminster Public Library.

CEMETERIES

A list of all the Cemeteries in the Metropolitan area, and the location of their records is readily available in *Greater London Cemeteries and Crematoria* (comp. P.S. Wolfston, revised C.R. Webb, Society of Genealogists, 1999), and this information is not therefore repeated here.

NONCONFORMIST RECORDS

London, as the capital, and largest centre of population, had (and has) an unrivalled collection of sects and chapels. It is only possible here to deal with the major ones, founded before 1837 and which left some records. Many ephemeral chapels either kept no records or any records which were kept have since been lost. In 1742, a General Registry for Protestant Dissenters was established, with its records kept by Dr. Williams's Library. When the Registry closed in 1837, due to the introduction of Civil Registration, its registers were surrendered and are now in the Public Record Office. Although intended to cover all England and Wales, naturally a particularly high proportion of entries came from the London and Middlesex area, due to the proximity of the Registry. There is an index to these entries on the CD Rom *Vital Records Index - British Isles*.

JEWS

The Jews had been expelled by Edward I in 1290, and only an occasional person with an apparently Jewish name is found from then until the mid-seventeenth century when, under the Commonwealth, a small settlement of Spanish and Portuguese Jews arrived in London. They were forced to live on the edge of the City since they were unable to join Livery companies until 1831, and were therefore forbidden the normal trades of the City. They were allowed to lease a Synagogue in Heneage Lane, and kept records (mainly in Portuguese until 1818). These were quite prosperous families in general and are known as Sephardic Jews.

The later seventeenth century saw the beginning of immigration of German and Polish or Ashkenasi Jews. The first London synagogue of this branch of Jewry was opened in Duke's Place in 1690, where it remained until destroyed by a bomb in 1940. Several other congregations followed. The records of these synagogues are usually written in Hebrew or Yiddish. The records of the various London Ashkenasi synagogues have mainly been collected centrally at United Synagogue, Woburn Place. The archives of the Western Synagogue in Westminster which was founded in 1761 are in the possession of that congregation.

For further details about Jewish registers, see *National Index of Parish Registers* 3, pp.957-977.

ROMAN CATHOLICS

A great many priests were at work in London in the eighteenth century. Priests could serve quite wide areas, since the diocesan system was not established until 1850, and the parochial not until World War I. Many of the earliest chapels were attached to embassies, and were primarily used for foreigners, though use was also made of them by local recusants.

Full and comprehensive details of pre-1880 Catholic missions and registers are to be found in a series by Michael Gandy, of which volume 1 covers London and the Home Counties. Only the briefest details of long-standing pre-1837 congregations are given, therefore, in this book.

INDEPENDENTS AND CONGREGATIONALISTS

Registers were surrendered by 77 Independent or Congragationalist chapels in Middlesex, and a further fourteen from the City.

The earliest register (Bull Lane, Stepney) dates from 1644. The only other seventeenth-century survivals are Brentford (1694) and Queen Street, Stepney (1698), and only two more (Bethnal Green, 1704 and St Clement Danes 1707) date from the first half of the eighteenth century. Twenty-two further registers start in the second half of the eighteenth century, the remainder from the first half of the nineteenth.

BAPTISTS

No early Baptist registers seem to survive for Middlesex. The earliest surrendered, Whitechapel, only dates from 1732, St George the Martyr in 1770 and Spitalfields in 1772, but there are no others until a clutch of register series starting in the 1780s (Hammersmith 1780; Shoreditch 1785; another Whitechapel 1786; Stepney 1786; Wapping 1786; St Luke Old Street 1787 and St Giles in the Fields 1788). Later pre-1837 foundations include Chelsea 1800; Stratford le Bow 1814; St Pancras 1820 and 1828 and Harrow 1831.

Just one Baptist register from the City was surrendered: Parliament Court, Bishopsgate, dating from 1795.

METHODISTS

Twenty-one Middlesex Methodist chapels surrendered registers and four more from the City. The earliest register is that at St Luke Old Street (1779) followed by Shoreditch (1788) and the Welsh Chapel in St Giles Cripplegate (1799). This last chapel had been founded in 1770. but there seems to be no records from the first thirty years of its existence. All other surrendered registers start in the nineteenth century.

Lady Huntingdon's Connexion later became part of the Methodist movement. Registers were surrendered by Clerkenwell (1778); St George in the East (1784); St Martin in the Fields (1790); Stepney (1791) and Lincolns Inn (1791).

Bible Christians were also later absorbed into the Methodists. A chapel in Shoreditch surrendered a register dating from 1823.

In 1818 the Wesleyan Methodists established a Metropolitan Registry in Paternoster Row for the registration of births and baptisms. When the registry was closed in 1837, it had recorded over 10,000 births and baptisms, which were surrendered and are now in the Public Record Office. There is an index to these entries on the CD Rom *Vital Records Index - British Isles.*

PRESBYTERIANS

Nine Middlesex Presbyterian chapels surrendered registers: Islington (1711); Enfield (1727); Scotch Church, Soho (1741); Whitechapel (1749); Hammersmith (1758); Hackney (1812); Kensington

(1814); St Clement Danes (1814) and St Marylebone (1825). Five more City Presbyterian congregations surrendered registers: Hand Alley, Bishopsgate (1705); Carter Lane, St Anne Blackfriars (1711); Meeting House Court, St Olave Old Jewry (1716); Miles Lane, St Michael Crooked Lane (1786) and Albion Chapel, St Giles Cripplegate (1817).

IRVINGITES

Six Middlesex Irvingite churches surrendered registers: Old Artillery Ground (1829); St Marylebone (1832); Chelsea (1834), Islington (1834); St John Westminster (1835) and Paddington (1835).

SWEDENBORGIANS

Swedenborgian registers were surrendered from St Anne Blackfriars (1787); Holborn (1797); Holborn (another) (1805) and St Giles in the Fields (1805).

SOCIETY OF FRIENDS (QUAKERS)

The Society of Friends was very active from the mid seventeenth century in London. Meeting houses with early surviving records are St Martin in the Fields (1644), Hammersmith (1648), South Mimms (1651), Stepney (1656), Tottenham (1662) and Harmondsworth (1662). The City Meeting House at Devonshire House only has registers from 1795.

The original registers are listed under their own section in the Public Record Office handlist, where the class reference RG 6. Before surrendering the registers the Society of Friends made 'Digests' of births, marriages and burials up to 1837 and as these are entered in volumes by surname, alphabetically in ten year chronological groups, they should be searched before the registers at the PRO. The applicable volumes of 'Digests' at the Society of Friends' Library covering the area now known as the 'Greater London Area' are marked 'London and Middlesex Quarterly Meeting' and cover:

C 1642-1837, M 1657-1737, B 1661-1837 and Supplement 1670-1836

Though listed under the ancient parish in which the meeting house was located, it will be convenient for searchers to have a single list of Quaker registers.

1. Quarterly Meeting (Inner & Outer Greater London Area)

Births:		Marriages:		Burials:	
498	1646-1707	1437	1658-1690	499	1661-1698
501		1293	Certs 1670-1719	331	1699-1722
328	1708-1747	497	1690-1704	330	1723-1758
329	1747-1775	496	1705-1727	500	1758-1775
966	1776-1780	495	1727-1775	975	1776-1779
971	1780-1786	965	1776-1794	973	1779-1783
972	1787-1794	1157	1795-1825	670	1783-1787
797	1795-1796	1158	1825-1836	1369	1788-1795
798	1797-1799			804	1795-1796
799	1800-1804			953	1797-1799
800	1805-1807			954	1799-1802
801	1808-1814			955	1803-1805
802	1814-1819			956	1806-1812
803	1820-1824			957	1812-1817
952	1825-1830			958	1817-1821
1045	1830-1835			1047	1822-1828
1046	1835-1837			1066	1828-1832
				1125	1832-1836
				1126	1836-1837

2. Registers of local Middlesex meetings.

a. Hammersmith

Baptisms:		Marriages:		Burials:	
1422	1648-1670	825	1633-1774	827	1665-1747
826	1652-1752	1422	1666-1670	1512	1676-1752
1516	1658-1750	1277	1685-1717	1442	1790-1808
836	1776-1793	1507	1688-1740	828	1747-1775
425	1790-1837	514	1777-1793	833	1776-1791
		540	1797-1837	829	1791-1794
				426	1795-1837

b. Tottenham (Hampstead End, Winchmore Hill, Barnet and South Mimms)

PRO: RG 6/1177: C 1651-1726; M 1675-1726; B 1666-1726

PRO: RG 6/1297, 840, 848, 506, 543, 549, 550: C 1727-1838; M 1727-1836; B 1726-1837

c. Westminster Monthly Meeting

PRO: RG 6/1490 Birth & Burial Notes 1678-1739

d. Peel Court, John Street, Westminster Meeting

Births:		Marriages:		Burials:	
1106	1644-1775	1079	1663-1773		1713-1745
1137	1644-1689	1436	1777-1794	1098	1668-1775
1563	1713-1739	536	1795-1836	591	1713-1762
1489	1717-1762			695	1776-1795
660	1775-1794			418	1795-1837
417	1795-1837				

e. Uxbridge (Longford & Staines)

PRO: RG 6/831, 838, 839, 525, 542, 547, 548: C 1662-1838, M 1670-1672, 1674-1790, 1795-1837, B 1672-1837

f. Ratcliff Monthly Meeting

Baptisms:		Marriages:		Burials:	
675	1656-1776	674	1657-1727	676	1666-1714
686	1775-1794	1400	1727-1775	1533	1714-1768
419	1795-1806	512	1776-1794	1534	1769-1776
		537	1795-1820	669	1776-1795
				420	1795-1821

3. City of London

a. Gracechurch Street Monthly Meeting

PRO: RG 6/415: C 1795-1837; RG 6/535: M 1795-1836; RG 6/416: B 1795-1837

b. Middlesex Quarterly Meeting: Devonshire House

Baptisms:		Marriages:		Burials:	
1102	1655-1747	974	1666-1707	673	1719-1776
1464	1699-1723	671	1707-1775	648	1776-1785
1103	1747-1776	510	1776-1794	811	785-1795
665	1775-1788	534	1795-1837	414	1795-1837
672	1782-1794				
413	1794-1837				

FOREIGN CHURCHES

London has always been a magnet for immigrant populations seeking to avoid persecution at home, or improve their economic lot. Immigrants before the middle of the eighteenth century (apart from the Jews) were mainly escapees from Catholic repression. Though they had their own churches, these conformed largely in practice to the Church of England, and their attendees were not regarded as Nonconformists, though it is convenient to deal with their records as though they were.

The largest collection of registers concern the Huguenots. Refugees from the Netherlands started arriving soon after the Reformation. Most of them worshipped at the Dutch Church in Austin Friars, whose registers begin in 1559, and which have been printed. Further waves of refugees from the Netherlands and France continued to arrive, the largest influx coming in the fifty years after the Revocation of the Edict of Nantes in 1685. Most of the refugees settled in a small number of areas, in London, principally Spitalfields and Soho. Their registers were surrendered and have been printed, with a great quantity of other material by the Huguenot Society of London.

A number of other foreign churches have surviving records, the Russian Orthodox church in St Marylebone being an early example, with registers dating from 1721. Others include the Swiss Church in Soho (registers from 1762) and the Greek Orthodox in St Stephen Coleman Street (registers from 1837).

In a similar category come the various Scotch churches. Again, since they represented the Established Church in Scotland, their attendees were not regarded as Nonconformists. Scotch church registers survive from St Margaret Lothbury (1689), Stepney (1741), St Margaret Westminster (1741), St Marylebone (1753), St Martin in the Fields (1794), St Pancras (1822) and Islington (1829).

Welsh churches, on the other hand, were Nonconformist (Calvinist Methodists) and are treated under the Methodists.

NEWSPAPERS

London and Middlesex are at the hub of English government, commerce and industry. Naturally, they have always had a very large number of newspapers, both local and national. For a guide the reader is referred to Jeremy Gibson's *Local Newspapers* 1750-1920 pp.33-38 (Federation of Family History Societies, 1987).

BIBLIOGRAPHY

Three recent bibliographies make any list here unnecessary. A full and comprehensive bibliography is provided by *Bibliography of Printed Works on London History to* 1939, Heather Creaton (Library Association, 1994). At a more popular level Stuart Raymond's *London and Middlesex: A Genealogical Bibliography* (Federation of Family History Societies, 2nd edition, 1998) provides the average user with all the references to printed material that is likely to be useful, while *Lists of Londoners*, Jeremy Gibson and Heather Creaton (Federation of Family History Societies, 1992) deals with unpublished material.

ABBREVIATIONS

Add Ms	Additional Manuscripts: British Library
b	built
B	Burials
BL	Department of Manuscripts, The British Library, London. A reader's ticket is necessary
Boyd	Marriage Index by P.Boyd. Copies at GL, SG and SLC. see NIPR Vol. 1
BT	Bishop's transcripts. For convenience this abbreviation is used for any annual register copy sent to an ecclesiastical superior
c	circa
C	Baptisms (also used for adult Baptisms of Baptists)
Ch Sec	Church or Chapel Secretary
C of A	College of Arms, Queen Victoria Street, London EC4V 4BT. The Library is not open to the public
Cop	Modern copies
CRS	Catholic Record Society publications
CRW	Copies in possession of author
D	Deaths
Dioc	Diocese
disc	discontinued
ELFHS	East of London Family History Society
Extr	Extracts
f	founded
fl	flourished
GL	Guildhall Library, Aldermanbury, London EC2P 2EJ.
I	Indexed
IGI	International Genealogical Index
Inc	Incumbent
K	Kelly's Directory
LMA	London Metropolitan Archives, 40 Northampton Road, London, EC1R 0HB
M	Marriages
Mf	Microfilm or microfiche
M Lic	Marriage Licences
Ms	Manuscript
NIPR	*National Index of Parish Registers*
NMFHS	London and North Middlesex Family History Society
N & Q	*Notes and Queries*
OR	Original Register
Phil Ms	Manuscript copies of parish registers in the possession of the Society of Genealogists
PRO	The Public Record Office, Ruskin Avenue, Kew, Richmond, Surrey TW9 4DK. A reader's ticket is necessary
Ptd	Printed
reb	rebuilt
SG	Society of Genealogists, 14 Charterhouse Buildings, Goswell Road, London EC1M 7BA. The Library is open to non-members on payment of hourly, half-daily and daily fees
SLC	The Genealogical Society of Utah, 35 North West Temple Street, Salt Lake City, Utah 84150, U.S.A.
Ts	Typescript
WMFHS	West Middlesex Family History Society
WMI	West Middlesex Marriage Index
WPL	City of Westminster Archives Centre, 10 St Ann's Street, SW1P 2XR
WSFHS	West Surrey Family History Society
Z	Births
+	Onwards. Invariably means 'until after 1837', and in the case of OR normally indicates that they continue to the present

ACTON St Mary, King Street (2,453) [Ossulstone Hundred; Brentford Union]
OR C 1539-1690, 1695-1936, M 1566-1689, 1695-1946, Banns 1760-1812,
  1912-40, B 1556-1684, 1695-1963 (LMA: DRO 52)
BT B 1664 (GL); 1801-02, 1804-30, 1832-33, CB 1852-53 (LMA)
Cop M 1566-1812 (Ptd, Phillimore 1, 1909); M 1566-1812 (Boyd); M 1813-37 (WMI);
  M 1566-1812 (I, SG)

ACTON Churchfield Street (United Reformed Church) f 1817
OR With Ch Sec

ACTON Roman Catholic Chapel (domestic chapel to Selby family) (Cath Dir 1828)
  closed 1856
OR C 1825+, M 1839+ (Inc Chiswick)

ASHFORD St Michael later **St Matthew**, Church Road (458) [Spelthorne Hundred;
  Staines Union] (transferred to Surrey 1965) (chapelry in Staines until 1859)
OR C 1699-1710, 1760-1905, M 1699-1708, 1754-1904, ML 1900-12,
  Banns 1754-1812, 1823-84, B 1700-10, 1760-1885 (LMA: DRO 78); CMB at Laleham
  1696-1810; CMB at Staines 1696-1710
BT 1629-30, 1639 (GL); 1800-41, 1846-60 (no M 1811, 1820, 1822-23, 1827, 1835,
  1837-41, 1846-58) (LMA)
Cop M 1696-1812 (Ptd, Phillimore 4, 1912); M 1629-30, 1813-37 (Ts GL, SG, CRW);
  M 1696-1710, 1760-1812 (Boyd); M 1813-37 (WMI); M 1790-1812 (Pallot Index)

BARNARD'S INN (in St Andrew Holborn) (Inn of Court) sold 1888

BARNET *see* **FRIERN BARNET**

BEDFONT, EAST St Mary, Hatton Road (968) [Spelthorne Hundred; Staines Union]
OR C 1678-1941, M 1695-1944, Banns 1820-1926, 1948-52, B 1678-1937 (LMA)
BT 1800-17, 1819, CB 1840-42 (LMA)
Cop C 1695-1851, M 1695-1860, B 1678-1852 (Ts SG); C 1678-1941, M 1695-1944,
  B 1678-1937 (LMA, Hounslow Lib, SG); M 1813-37 (WMI)

BETHNAL GREEN Brady Street Cemetery, Brady Street (Jewish)
OR B 1761-1858 (United Synagogue Burial Society, Upper Woburn Place, WC1)

BETHNAL GREEN Gibraltar Burial Ground (Dissenters Burial Ground)
OR B 1793-1837 (PRO: RG 8/305-315)
Cop B 1793-1837 (Ts I PRO)

BETHNAL GREEN St Matthew, St Matthew's Row (62,018) [Ossulstone Hundred;
  Bethnal Green Union] (created from Stepney, 1746; transferred to London, 1889)
OR C 1746-1964, M 1746-1976, B 1746-1977 (LMA)
BT 1802-13, 1829-57, 1859-62 (no C 1802, no M 1841-62, no B 1854-62) (LMA)
Cop C 1746-78, 1794-99, 1803-08, 1813-19, 1822-37, M 1746-1837, Banns 1754-65
  (Ts I only, SG); M 1746-66 (SG); M 1829-37, Banns 1754-65 (Ts I only, SG)

BETHNAL GREEN St John, Bethnal Green (created from Bethnal Green, 1837)
OR C 1837-1931, M 1837-1938, B 1847-55 (LMA)

BETHNAL GREEN Independent Chapel, Cambridge Road f 1662 or earlier
OR ZC 1704-55, 1771-1836, 1845-58 (PRO: RG 4/4137, 4178, 4577)
Cop C 1771-1836 (SG)

BETHNAL GREEN Domestic Mission Chapel, Spicer Street (Presbyterian) f 1832 b 1836
  moved to Mansford Street 1889
OR C 1832+ (Ch Sec)

BETHNAL GREEN Sydney Street (Independent)
OR C 1846-80 (PRO: RG 8/31-32)

BETHNAL GREEN Virginia Chapel (Independent)
OR C 1825-37 (PRO: RG 8/33)
Cop C 1825-37 (Ts CRW, SG)

BLOOMSBURY St George, Bloomsbury Way (16,475) [Ossulstone Hundred;
  St Giles in the Fields and St George Bloomsbury Union] (transferred to London, 1889)
  (created from St Giles in the Fields, 1731)
OR C 1730-1918, M 1730-1927, B 1730-1855 (LMA)
BT 1800-11, 1813-37 (LMA)
Cop C 1775-1838 (Ts I only, SG)

BRENTFORD, NEW St Lawrence (2,036) [Elthorne Hundred; Brentford Union]
  (chapelry in Hanwell until 1721)
OR C 1620, 1653-59, 1665-1961, M 1618-40, 1654-58, 1666-1961, Banns 1653-1721,
  1754-1810, 1824-1961, B 1570-1843, (LMA: DRO 58)
BT 1629-30, 1639 (GL); 1800-15, 1817-58. 1860-64 (no M 1837, 1842-64) (LMA)
Cop M 1618-1812 (Ptd, Phillimore 4, 1912); C 1619-20, 1653-1805, 1618-1905 (SG);
  M 1618-1812 (Boyd); M 1790-1812 (Pallot Index); M 1813-36 (Ts I GL, LMA, SG,
  CRW); C 1570-1805, M 1570-1754, 1813-36, B 1570-1805 (LMA); M 1813-36 (WMI)

BRENTFORD, NEW Albany Chapel later Brentford Congregational Church, Boston Road
  f 1693
OR ZC 1694-1865, B 1786-94, 1800-62 (defective) (LMA: N/C/34)
Cop (Mf) ZC 1785-1820, 1831-37, B 1785-1826 (SG)

BRENTFORD, NEW Park Church, Boston Manor Road (Baptist) f 1802
OR no registers known

BRENTFORD, NEW North Road Chapel (Particular Baptist) f 1819
OR no registers known

BRENTFORD, OLD St George [Brentford Union] (chapelry in Ealing until 1828)
OR C 1828-1959, M 1837-1959, Banns 1837-1959, B 1828-67 (LMA: DRO 59)
BT M 1808, CB 1828, 1830-49, 1851-60, 1862-68 (no B 1858-59, 1862-68), CB 1829
  (filed under Ealing) (LMA)

BROMLEY ST LEONARD St Mary, Bromley High Street (4, 846) [Ossulstone Hundred;
  Poplar Union] (transferred to London, 1889)
OR CM 1622-1960, B 1622-1866 (LMA)
BT 1639 (GL); Apr 1803-Apr 1804, May 1805-May 1806, May 1808-94 (no M 1837-94,
  no B 1857-94) (LMA)
Cop C 1786-1838, M 1755-1837 (Ts I only SG); M 1639 (Ts I GL, LMA, SG, CRW)

BUCKINGHAM PALACE (extra-parochial)

BUNHILL FIELDS *see* **ST LUKE OLD STREET**

CHARTERHOUSE Burial Ground
OR B 1815-1911 (LMA: acc.1876)

CHARTERHOUSE St Mary alias **SUTTON'S HOSPITAL**, Charterhouse Square, EC1M 6AN (extra-parochial area, later in St Luke Old Street) (164) [Ossulstone Hundred; Holborn Union] (transferred to London, 1889)
OR C 1696+, M 1671-1754, 1837+, B 1695-1854 (Inc)
BT CB 1813-35 (LMA: under Sutton's.Hospital)
Cop C 1696-1836, M 1671-1754, 1837-90, B 1695-1854 (Ptd, HS 18, 1892);
    C 1696-1836, M 1671-1754, 1837-76 (IGI); M 1671-1754 (Boyd); B 1813-53 (CLBI)

CHELSEA Western Cemetery, Fulham Road (Jewish)
OR B 1815-84 (Western Marble Arch Synagogue Burial Society, Great Cumberland Place) (some registers destroyed by enemy action, 1941)

CHELSEA Royal Hospital Chapel, Royal Hospital Road
OR C 1691-1812, M 1691-1765, B 1692-1856 (PRO: RG 4/4330, 4332, 4387);
    C 1813+ (Chaplain)
BT CB 1813-59 (no C 1843, no B 1857-59) (LMA)
Cop C 1692-1812, M 1691-1753 (C of A); M 1701-65 (Boyd);
    C 1692-1796, M 1691-1765 (IGI)

CHELSEA St Luke, Sydney Street (32,371) [Ossulstone Hundred; Chelsea Union] (transferred to London, 1889)
OR C 1559-1925, M 1559-1958, B 1559-1883 (LMA); B (sexton's books) 1756-78 (Chelsea Lib)
BT 1639, 1752 (GL); 1745-56 (no M 1755-56), 1803-60 (no Apr 1805-Feb 1807, 1853, no M 1838-60, no B 1841-60) (LMA)
Cop M 1704-60 (Ptd, J.S.W. Gibson, 1958); C 1813-18, M 1761-1800 (SG);
    M 1701-54 (Boyd); C 1778-1837, M 1704-1837, B 1830-39 (Ts I only, SG); M 1639, 1752 (Ts I GL, LMA, SG, CRW)

CHELSEA Holy Trinity, Sloane Street
OR C 1832-1959, M 1832-1952, B 1832-35 (LMA)
BT 1832-40, 1842-59 (no MB 1838-59) (LMA)
Cop C 1832-37, M 1832-37 (Ts I only, SG); B 1832-35 (Ts SG)

CHELSEA French Church, Little Chelsea *fl. c*1700
OR no registers known

CHELSEA French Church, Cook's Ground *fl. c*1700
OR no registers known

CHELSEA Independent Chapel, Cook's Ground f 1772
OR ZC 1772-81, 1786-1827 (PRO: RG 4/4179, 4386)

CHELSEA Presbyterian Church
OR C 1803-44 (Presbyterian Historical Society)

CHELSEA Union Chapel, New Road, Sloane Street (Independent) f 1800
OR C 1835-36 (PRO: RG 4/4385)

CHELSEA Baptist Chapel, Paradise Row f 1800
OR B 1800-36 (PRO: RG 4/4142)

CHELSEA St Mary, Cadogan Street (Roman Catholic) f 1798 (Cath Dir 1965)
OR C 1798-1814 (Archives de Nantes); C 1804+, M 1814+, Banns 1858+,
    B 1845-58 (Inc)
Cop M 1837-70 (I Institute of Heraldic & Genealogical Studies, Canterbury);
    B 1845-68 (Catholic FHS)

CHELSEA Wesleyan Chapel, Sloane Terrace f 1811
OR ZC 1810-37 (PRO: RG 4/4329)

CHELSEA Ranelagh Chapel (Calvinist Methodist) f 1814
OR ZC 1814-37 (PRO: RG 4/4261)

CHELSEA Jewish Cemetery, Queen's Elm Parade, Fulham Road opened 1815,
   closed 1885
OR no registers known

CHELSEA Irvingite Church, College Street f 1832
OR Z 1835-37, C 1834-40 (PRO: RG 4/4143, 4180, 4299)

CHISWICK St Nicholas, Church Street (4,994) [Ossulstone Hundred; Brentford Union]
OR CMB 1678+, Banns 1955+ (Inc)
BT 1813-55 (no M 1838-55, B 1855) (LMA)
Cop M 1678-1800 (Ptd, W.P.W. Phillimore and W.H. Whitear, 1897); C 1678-1872,
   M 1800-37, B 1678-1850 (I SG); C 1678-1851, M 1678-1837, B 1678-1850 (Ts I SG);
   M 1678-1800 (Boyd); M 1790-1837 (Pallot Index)

CLEMENT'S INN (in St Clement Danes) (Inn of Court)

CLERKENWELL St James, Clerkenwell Green (47,634 incl.St John) [Ossulstone
   Hundred; Holborn Union] (transferred to London, 1889)
OR C 1561-1926, M 1587-1945, Banns 1762-1840, 1846-75, B 1561-1853 (LMA)
BT 1807-40 (no M 1838-40) (LMA)
Cop C 1551-1700 (Ptd, HS 9, 1884); C 1701-54 (Ptd, HS 10, 1885); M 1551-1754 (Ptd,
   HS 13, 1887); B 1551-1665 (Ptd, HS 17, 1891); B 1666-1719 (Ptd, HS 19, 1893);
   B 1720-54 (Ptd, HS 20, 1894); C 1754-1837, M 1754-1837 (Ts I only, SG);
   M 1551-1754 (Boyd)

CLERKENWELL St John the Baptist, St John's Square [Ossulstone Hundred; Holborn
   Union] (transferred to London, 1889) (Priory church, separate parish 1723)
OR C 1723-1930, M 1723-1929, B 1723-1853 (LMA)
BT 1807-12, 1814-37 (LMA)
Cop C 1723-1838, M 1723-1838 (Ts I only, SG)

CLERKENWELL St Mark, Myddelton Square (created from Clerkenwell St James, 1829)
   (transferred to London, 1889)
OR C 1828-1930, M 1839-1931, B 1830-56 (LMA)
Cop C 1828-40, B 1830-56 (Ts I GL, LMA, SG, CRW)

CLERKENWELL Pentonville Chapel alias **St James**, Pentonville Road (created from
   Clerkenwell St James, 1862)
OR C 1790-1977, M 1847-1977, B 1790-1855 (LMA)
BT CB 1813-26 (LMA)
Cop B 1790-97 (Ts I GL, LMA, SG, CRW); B 1788-1855 (LMA, SG)
Cop (Mf) C 1810-76 (SG)

CLERKENWELL St Philip, Granville Square (created from Clerkenwell
   St Mark Myddleton Square, 1840)
OR C 1834-1935, M 1847-1935 (LMA)

CLERKENWELL Spa Fields Chapel (Lady Huntingdon's Connexion) f 1777
OR ZC 1783-1837, B 1778-1849 (PRO: RG 4/4171, 4208-09, 4316-22, 4366-67, 4536)
   (Index to burials in progress)

CLERKENWELL Claremont Chapel, Pentonville (now Claremont Central Mission, White Lion Street) (Independent) f 1819
OR ZC 1819-37 (PRO: RG 4/4282)

CLERKENWELL Providence Chapel, Chadwell Street (became Northampton Tabernacle, Upper Rosoman Street, 1835)
OR C 1835-45 (PRO: RG 8/39)
Cop C 1835-37 (Ts GL, SG)

CLERKENWELL Wilderness Row Wesleyan Methodist Chapel
OR ZC 1824-37 (PRO: RG 4/4266)
Cop C 1824-37 (Ts GL, SG); C 1799-1875 (Ts SG)

CLERKENWELL Rawstone Street Chapel, Goswell Road
OR C 1830-37 (PRO: RG 8/40)

CLIFFORD'S INN (extra-parochial) (Inn of Court) sold 1903

COLNBROOK St Thomas (part in Middlesex, part in Buckinghamshire) (created from Langley Marish chapelry in Wraysbury parish, Horton, Buckinghamshire and Stanwell, Middlesex, 1853)
OR C 1760-1957, M 1852-1957, Banns 1880-1959, B 1852-1933 (Bucks RO)
BT 1633, 1813-33 (Bucks RO); 1851 (Oxfordshire Archives)
Cop C 1760-1877, M 1852-77 (Bucks IGI)
Cop (Mf) C 1760-1924, M 1852-1948, Banns 1880-1923, B 1852-1933 (Bucks RO);
   C 1760-1875, MB 1852-75 (SLC)

COVENT GARDEN St Paul (5,203) [City of Westminster; Strand Union] (created from St Martin in the Fields, 1645) (transferred to London, 1889)
OR C 1653-1945, M 1653-1963, Banns 1653-1972, B 1653-1853 (WPL)
BT 1800-35 (LMA)
Cop C 1653-1752 (Ptd, HS 33, 1906; C 1752-1837 (Ptd, HS 34, 1906);
   M 1653-1837 (Ptd, HS 35, 1906); B 1653-1752 (Ptd, HS 36, 1908); B 1752-1853 (Ptd, HS 37, 1909); M 1653-1837 (Boyd)

COWLEY St Laurence, Church Road (315) [Elthorne Hundred; Uxbridge Union]
OR C 1562-1949, M 1563-1947, B 1562-1938 (LMA: DRO 22)
BT 1629-30, 1639 (GL); 1800-09, 1813, 1821-76, 1878-79 (no M 1838-79) (LMA)
Cop M 1563-1812 (Ptd, Phillimore 2, 1910); M 1629-30, 1639 (Ts I GL, LMA, SG, CRW); M 1563-1812 (Boyd); M 1790-1837 (Pallot Index)

CRANFORD ST JOHN St Dunstan, Cranford Park (377) [Elthorne Hundred; Staines Union]
OR C 1564-1996, M 1564-1834, ML 1834, Banns 1821-1936, B 1564-1996
   (LMA: DRO 9)
BT 1629-30, 1639 (GL); 1800-Apr 1809, Apr 1810-15, CB 1837-43, 1847-48 (LMA)
Cop M 1564-1834 (Ts I GL, LMA, SG, CRW); M 1813-37 (Pallot Index)

DRAYTON, WEST St Martin, Church Road (662) [Elthorne Hundred; Uxbridge Union]
   (Peculiar of the Dean and Chapter of St Paul's until 1845)
OR C 1568-1977, M 1570-1979, Banns 1755-1812, 1969-75, B 1571-1927
   (LMA: DRO 1)
BT 1813-24, 1826-36 (no M 1817, 1821, 1829), CB 1860 (LMA)
Cop M 1568-1812 (Ptd Phillimore 2, 1910); M 1813-37 (Ts I GL, LMA, SG, CRW);
   M 1568-1813 (Boyd); M 1813-37 (WMI)
Cop (Mf) C 1568-1701, B 1570-1706 (SG)

DRAYTON, WEST Particular Baptist Chapel, Money Lane, f 1827
  rebuilt in Swan Road 1925
OR no registers known

EALING St Mary, St Mary's Road (7,783) [Ossulstone Hundred; Brentford Union]
OR C 1582-1968, M 1582-1979, ML 1764, Banns 1774-1984, B 1582-1962
  (LMA: DRO 37)
BT 1630, 1639, 1663 (GL); 1801-08, 1810-69 (no M 1838-69) (LMA)
Cop M 1582-1837 (Ptd Phillimore 8, 1927); M 1630, 1639, 1663 (Ts I GL, LMA, SG,
CRW); M 1582-1775, 1801-37 (Boyd); M 1790-1837 (Pallot Index); M 1582-1837 (I, SG)

EALING Ealing Green Independent Chapel, Ealing Green f 1800
OR no registers known

EALING Albany Independent Chapel, Old Brentford f 1829
OR C 1831-37 (PRO: RG 4/370)
Cop C 1831-37 (Ptd Mf, CRW and NMFHS, 1985)
Cop (Mf) C 1831-37 (SLC)

EDGWARE St Margaret, Station Road (591) [Gore Hundred; Hendon Union]
OR C 1717-1857, M 1717-1840, Banns 1754-1812, B 1717-1867 (LMA: DRO 11)
BT 1630, 1639 (GL); 1800-14, 1816-44, 1846-66, 1868 (no M 1835-42, 1846, 1853-68)
  (LMA)
Cop M 1630, 1717-1837 (Ts I GL, LMA, SG, CRW)

EDMONTON All Saints, Church Street (8,192) [Edmonton Hundred; Edmonton Union]
OR C 1558-1859, M 1558-1892, Banns 1754-1921, B 1557-1882 (LMA: DRO 10)
BT 1629 (GL); 1800-09, 1813-36 (LMA)
Cop M 1557-1837 (Ptd Phillimore 6, 1914); C 1558-1715, B 1557-1727
  (SG, Bpsgate Lib); M 1629 (Ts I GL, LMA, SG, CRW)

EDMONTON Weld Chapel, later Christ Church, Southgate (created from
  Edmonton All Saints, 1851)
OR C 1695-1812, M 1702-54, B 1695-1812 (LMA: DRO 65); C 1813-1949,
  M 1838-1953, B 1813-1939, Funerals 1913-55 (LMA: DRO 40)
BT included in Edmonton All Saints 1813-36

EDMONTON St Paul, Winchmore Hill (chapel, Edmonton All Saints, made parish, 1851)
OR C 1834-75 (LMA); M 1842+ (Inc)

EDMONTON Glass House Memorial Church, Winchmore Hill (Baptist) f 1680
OR no registers known

EDMONTON Winchmore Hill Chapel (Independent) f 1773
OR ZC 1819-37, B 1831-32 (PRO: RG 4/2458)
Cop ZC 1819-37, B 1831-32 (Ptd Mf, CRW and NMFHS, 1985)
Cop (Mf) ZC 1819-37, B 1831-32 (SG, SLC)

EDMONTON Edmonton and Tottenham Chapels, Fore Street (Independent) f 1789
OR C 1802-09, 1818-80, B 1792-1809, 1826, 1879, 1903 (LMA: N/C/64);
  ZC 1818, 1830-37, B 1821-36 (PRO: RG 4/371-372)
Cop ZC 1818, 1830-37, B 1821-36 (Ptd Mf, CRW and NMFHS, 1985)
Cop (Mf) ZC 1818, 1830-37, B 1821-36 (SG, SLC)

EDMONTON Chase Side Chapel, Southgate f 1806
OR ZC 1812-36 (PRO: RG 4/2045)
Cop ZC 1812-36 (Ptd Mf, CRW and NMFHS, 1985)
Cop (Mf) ZC 1812-36 (SLC)

ENFIELD St Andrew, Market Place (8,812) [Edmonton Hundred; Edmonton Union]
OR CM 1550-1981, Banns 1896-1901, 1906-83, B 1550-1928, 1945-66 (LMA: DRO 4)
BT 1800-51 (no M 1838-51) (LMA)
Cop M 1550-1837 (Ptd Phillimore 5, 1914)

ENFIELD Jesus Church, Bulls Cross, Forty Hill (created from Enfield St Andrew, 1845)
OR C 1835-1937, M 1847-1939 (LMA: DRO 46)
BT C 1846-47 (LMA)

ENFIELD HIGHWAY St James (created from Enfield St Andrew, 1832)
OR C 1834-1951, M 1845-1955, B 1834-1957 (LMA: DRO 54)
BT CB 1834-42 in Enfield St Andrew returns; CB 1842-51 (LMA)

ENFIELD Baker Street Meeting (Presbyterian) f 1662
OR ZC 1727-1837 (PRO: RG 4/1129)
Cop ZC 1727-1837 (Ptd Mf, CRW and NMFHS, 1985)
Cop (Mf) ZC 1727-1837 (SG, SLC)

ENFIELD Chapel, High Street, Ponder's End (Independent) f 1757
OR ZC 1783-1800, 1805-36 (PRO: RG 4/2459-2460); ZC 1769-77, 1781, 1801-03 (minute
   book) (Ch Sec)
Cop ZC 1783-1800, 1805-36 (Ptd Mf, CRW and NMFHS, 1985); ZC 1769-77, 1781,
   1801-03 (minute book) (Ts SG)
Cop (Mf) ZC 1783-1800, 1805-36 (SG, SLC)

ENFIELD Christ Church, Chase Side (Independent) f 1780
OR ZC 1808-36 (PRO: RG 4/1128); ZC 1790-1871, B 1831-54 (PRO: RG 8/79)
Cop ZC 1790-1840, B 1831-54 (Ptd Mf, CRW and NMFHS, 1985)
Cop (Mf) ZC 1808-36, B 1831-54 (SG, SLC)

ENFIELD Highway (Independent) f 1820
OR C 1830-38 (PRO: RG 4/1130)
Cop C 1830-38 (Ptd Mf, CRW and NMFHS, 1985)
Cop (Mf) C 1830-38 (SG, SLC)

FELTHAM St Dunstan with St Catherine (924) [Spelthorne Hundred; Staines Union]
OR C 1634-1907, M 1634-58, 1669-1893, B 1634-59, 1695-1900 (LMA: DRO 13)
BT 1639 (GL); 1800-06, 1813-17, 1819, 1821-67 (LMA)
Cop M 1634-1812 (Ptd Phillimore 4, 1912); M 1813-37 (Ts I GL, LMA, SG,
   CRW); M 1634-1812 (Boyd); M 1813-37 (WMI); M 1634-1812 (I, SG); M 1790-1837
   (Pallot Index); CM 1813-75 (IGI)

FINCHLEY St Mary (3,210), Hendon Lane, Church End [Ossulstone Hundred;
   Barnet Union]
OR C 1560-1948, M 1561-1958, Banns 1754-1812, B 1558-1911 (LMA: DRO 32);
   Banns 1823-1903, 1910-60 (Inc)
BT 1800-07, 1809-10, 1812-14, 1816-37 (LMA)
Cop M 1561-1837 (Ptd Phillimore 7, 1915)

FINCHLEY St John the Apostle, Whetstone (created from Finchley, 1833)
OR C 1834-1968, M 1848-1973, Banns 1958-70, B 1835-1922 (LMA: DRO 57)
Cop C 1834-60 (Ts SG)

FINCHLEY Whetstone Chapel, Oakleigh Road North (Independent)
OR ZC 1788-1804, 1819, 1831-37, B 1800, 1835-37 (PRO: RG 4/1134)
Cop ZC 1788-1804, 1819, 1831-37, B 1800, 1835-37 (Ptd Mf, CRW and NMFHS, 1985)
Cop (Mf) ZC 1788-1804, 1819, 1831-37, B 1800, 1835-37 (SG, SLC)

FINCHLEY Soho Memorial Church, High Road (Baptist) f 1791
OR no registers known

FINCHLEY East Finchley Independent Chapel, High Road f 1815
OR no registers known

FRIERN BARNET St James, Friern Barnet Lane (615) [Ossulstone Hundred;
   Barnet Union] (chapel of ease to Clerkenwell Priory until 1549)
OR C 1673-1963, M 1675-1974, Banns 1812-75, 1890-1978, B 1674-1927
   (LMA: DRO 12)
BT 1813-37 (no M 1814, 1819), CB 1840-41, 1849 (LMA)
Cop M 1675-1837 (Ts I GL, LMA, SG, CRW)

FULHAM All Saints, Church Gate (17,537) [Ossulstone Hundred; Fulham Union]
   (transferred to London, 1889)
OR C 1675-1923, M 1675-1946, B 1675-1863 (LMA)
BT 1614 (GL); 1800, 1802-36 (LMA)
Cop M 1614 (Ts I GL, LMA, SG, CRW); C 1828-32 (I SG)
Cop (Mf) C 1675-1979, M 1675-1937, B 1675-1863 (Hammersmith and Fulham Archives)

FULHAM St John, North End Road, Walham Green (created from Fulham All Saints,
   1835)
OR C 1836-1954, M 1837-1957, B 1836-53 (LMA); C 1954+, M 1957+ (Inc)
Cop B 1836-53 (Ts SG)

FULHAM St Mary, Hammersmith Road (created from Fulham All Saints, 1835)
OR C 1836-1960, M 1837-1943, B 1836-89 (LMA)
Cop B 1836-89 (Ts I SG)

FURNIVAL'S INN (160) (extra-parochial place) (Inn of Court) [Ossulstone Hundred;
   Holborn Union] (transferred to London, 1889)

GLASSHOUSE YARD, Liberty of (1,312) (extra-parochial liberty adjoining St Botolph
   Aldersgate and incorporated therein 1685) [Ossulstone Hundred; East London Union
   1866-69, City Union 1869-89, Holborn Union 1889-1930] (transferred to London,
   1889)

GRAY'S INN Chapel, Gray's Inn Square (324) (extra-parochial place) (Inn of Court)
   [Ossulstone Hundred; Holborn Union] (transferred to London, 1889)
OR C 1705+, M 1695-1754, 1850+ (Chaplain)
Cop M 1695-1754 (Ptd, J. Foster, 1889); M 1695-1754 (Boyd); C 1705-1862,
   M 1695-1850 (possibly extracts only) (Ms SG)

GREENFORD Holy Cross, Ferrymead Gardens (477) [Elthorne Hundred;
   Brentford Union]
OR CMB 1539+, Banns 1754-99, 1836-1929, 1935+ (Inc)
BT 1629-30 (GL); 1800-09, 1822-46 (no M May 1841-42, 1845) (LMA)
Cop M 1539-1812 (Ptd, Phillimore 1, 1909)

HACKNEY Cemetery formerly **Grove Street Cemetery**, Lauriston Road (Jewish)
OR B 1788-1886 (United Synagogue Burial Society, Upper Woburn Place, WC1)

HACKNEY St Thomas Square Cemetery, Mare Street
OR B 1837-76 (PRO: RG 8/41)

HACKNEY Abney Park Cemetery, Stoke Newington High Street
OR B 1840-1978 (Hackney Archives Department)
Cop (Mf) B 1840-1978 (Hackney Archives Department)

HACKNEY St John at (31,047) [Ossulstone Hundred; Hackney Union] (transferred to London, 1889)
OR C 1545-1952, M 1589-1968, B 1593-1933 (LMA)
BT 1800-55 (no M 1838-55) (LMA)
Cop C 1545-46, 1555-1812, M 1589-1754, B 1593-1812 (Ms GL, SG); C 1545-1899,
   M 1589-1837, B 1737-69, 1831-37 (I SG); M 1738-54, B 1738-69 (Ts SG);
   C 1555-1823, M 1593-1832, B 1593-1819 (Ms Hackney Archives Dept); M 1589-1754
   (Boyd); CB 1821-99 (I SG)

HACKNEY St John of Jerusalem, Lauriston Road (created from St John at Hackney,
   1825) (transferred to London, 1889)
OR C 1826-1957, M 1831-1958, B 1831-1924 (LMA); C 1957+, M 1958+ (Inc)
BT 1826-56 (no M 1838-56) (LMA)

HACKNEY St Thomas, Clapton Common (formerly **Stamford Hill Chapel**) (created from
   St John at Hackney, 1825) (transferred to London, 1889)
OR C 1827-1935, M 1831-1939 (LMA)
BT 1827-46 (no M 1838-46) (LMA)

HACKNEY St Barnabas with St Paul, Stoke Newington Road, West Hackney (created
   from St John at Hackney, 1824) (transferred to London, 1889)
OR C 1824-1911, M 1824-1924, B 1824-88 (LMA); C 1911+, M 1924+ (Inc)
BT 1824-41 (no M 1838-41) (LMA)
Cop C 1828-37, M 1824-37 (Ts I only, SG)

HACKNEY Dalston Independent Chapel, Middleton Road f 1662
OR no registers known

HACKNEY Pownall Road Chapel (Independent) f 18th C (now united to
   Middleton Road Chapel)
OR no registers known

HACKNEY Mare Street (Presbyterian) f 1665 b 1668 moved to Gravel Pit 1716;
   New Gravel Pit 1858-1969
OR B 1812-37 (PRO: RG 4/4244-45)

HACKNEY St Thomas' Square Chapel, Mare Street f 1672 closed 1896 (Presbyterian)
OR Z 1787-91, 1814-37, C 1765-1837, B 1787-1837 (PRO: RG 4/4307-08, 4186, 4434);
   B 1837-76 (PRO: RG 8/41); admissions 1766-1828, C 1814-98, M 1838-48, some B in
   members lists (Hackney Archives Dept)

HACKNEY Baptist Chapel, Frampton Park Road, Mare Street (Baptist) f 1798
OR no registers known

HACKNEY Independent Chapel, Well Street f 1800
OR ZC 1837 (PRO: RG 4/4398)

HACKNEY Old Gravel Pit Meeting House (Independent) f 1803
OR ZC 1802-37 (PRO: RG 4/4336)

HACKNEY Clapton Independent Chapel, Lower Clapton Road f 1804
OR no registers known

HACKNEY The New Chapel, Upper Clapton Road (Independent) f 1812
OR ZC 1827-37 (PRO: RG 4/4144)

HACKNEY Pleasant Place Chapel (Wesleyan Methodist) f 1816
OR ZC 1818-37 (PRO: RG 4/4245)

HACKNEY Trinity Chapel, Lauriston Road, South Hackney (Independent) f 1823
OR no registers known

HADLEY, MONKEN St Mary the Virgin (979) [Edmonton Hundred; Barnet Union]
(transferred to Hertfordshire, 1904)
OR C 1619-1941, M 1619-1956, Banns 1757-1953, B 1619-1952 (LMA: DRO 17)
BT 1639 (GL); 1805-74, 1876-78, 1880-84 (no M 1840-41, 1843-84) (LMA)
Cop M 1639 (Ts I GL, LMA, SG, CRW); B 1775-1952 (Ts I SG)
Cop (Mf) B 1775-1952 (SG)

HAMMERSMITH St Paul, Queen Caroline Street (10,222) [Ossulstone Hundred;
Kensington Union 1837-45, Fulham Union 1845-1930] (chapelry of Fulham until 1631)
(transferred to London, 1889)
OR C 1664-73, 1682-1700, 1707-28, 1733-1960, M 1664-73, 1683-89, 1697-1702,
1707-27, 1734-36, 1748-1972, Banns 1838-1962, B 1664-73, 1682-1700, 1704-28,
1733-1854 (Hammersmith and Fulham Archives)
BT 1801-02, 1804-26 (LMA)
Cop CMB 1664-71 (Ts GL, Hammersmith and Fulham Archives)

HAMMERSMITH St Peter, Black Lion Yard (created from St Paul Hammersmith, 1836)
OR C 1836-1965, M 1836-1941, B 1832-55 (LMA)
Cop M 1836-37 (Ts CRW); B 1832-55 (Ts I SG)

HAMMERSMITH White Horse Chapel later **George Yard Chapel**, Broadway
(Independent formerly Presbyterian) f 1650
OR C 1758-1837 (PRO: RG 4/375, 2203, 3595)
Cop C 1758-1837 (Ptd Mf, CRW and NMFHS, 1985)
Cop (Mf) C 1758-1837 (SLC)

HAMMERSMITH Meeting House, Lower Mall (Society of Friends)
(registers listed more fully in introduction)
OR Z 1648-1752, 1776-1837, M 1663-1774, 1777-93, 1797-1837, B 1676-1808
(PRO: RG 6/425-26, 514, 540, 825-29, 833, 836, 1277, 1422, 1442, 1507, 1512,
1516)
Cop Z 1648-1752, 1776-1837, M 1663-1774, 1777-93, 1797-1837, B 1676-1808
(Friends' House)

HAMMERSMITH Roman Catholic Chapel, King Street f 1674 (in 1853 chapel moved to
Brook Green, as Holy Trinity Brook Green)
OR C 1710-1838 (Westminster Diocesan Archives), C 1856+, M 1845+ (Inc)
Cop C 1710-1838 (Ptd, CRS 26, 1926); C 1710-1838 (IGI); M 1851-70 (I Institute of
Heraldic & Genealogical Studies, Canterbury)

HAMMERSMITH Ebenezer Chapel (Independent) f 1773
OR ZC 1773-1835, B 1786-87 (PRO: RG 4/374)
Cop ZC 1773-1835, B 1786-87 (Ptd Mf, CRW and NMFHS, 1985)
Cop (Mf) ZC 1773-1835, B 1786-87 (SLC)

HAMMERSMITH Trinity Chapel, West End, King Street (Baptist) f 1783
OR Z 1780-1837, B 1784-1837 (PRO: RG 4/373, 2914)
Cop Z 1780-1837, B 1784-1837 (Ptd Mf, CRW and NMFHS, 1985)
Cop (Mf) Z 1780-1837, B 1784-1837 (SLC)

HAMMERSMITH Wesleyan Chapel, Waterloo Street (Wesleyan Methodist) f 1809
OR ZC 1807-37, B 1814-54 (PRO: RG 4/1943-45)
Cop ZC 1807-37, B 1814-54 (Ptd Mf, CRW and NMFHS, 1985)
Cop (Mf) ZC 1807-37, B 1814-54 (SLC)

HAMPSTEAD St John, Church Row (7,263) [Ossulstone Hundred; Edmonton Union 1837-48, Hampstead Parish 1848-1930] (transferred to London, 1889)
OR C 1600+, M 1601+, B 1560+ (Inc)
BT 1639 (GL); 1800-09 (LMA)
Cop M 1639 (Ts I GL, LMA, SG, CRW); Extr C 1600-1747, M 1601-1750, B 1560-1773 (SG)
Cop (Mf) C 1600-1840, M 1601-1837, B 1560-1842 (Holborn Library)

HAMPSTEAD Red Lion Hill (Presbyterian) f 1687 b 1691 moved to Rosslyn Hill, 1862

HAMPSTEAD St Mary, Holly Place, Church Row (Roman Catholic) f 1796
OR C 1800-96, M 1838-1903, D 1817-1900 (Westminster Diocesan Archives); C 1896+, M 1903+ (Inc)
Cop C 1800-96, M 1838-1903, B 1817-1909 (Ts I SG)

HAMPTON St Mary (3,992) [Spelthorne Hundred; Kingston Union]
OR C 1554-1904, M 1657-1703, 1726-1903, Banns 1803-28, B 1554-1650, 1656-77, 1723-1973 (LMA: DRO 140)
BT 1629, 1639 (GL); 1800-60 (no M 1840-60) (LMA)
Cop M 1657-1812 (Ptd, Phillimore 3, 1911); C 1554-1704, 1724-25, 1749-1812, M 1657-1837, B 1554-1650, 1656-77, 1723-25, 1749-1812 (Ts I SG); C 1554-1704, 1724-1812, B 1554-1677, 1723-1812 (Ts SG); M 1629, 1639. 1813-37 (Ts I GL, LMA, SG, CRW); M 1657-1812 (Boyd); M 1790-1837 (Pallot Index); M 1813-37 (WMI)

HAMPTON WICK St John the Baptist (1, 463) (created from Hampton St Mary, 1831)
OR C 1831-1967, M 1832-1955, Banns 1832-1975 (LMA: DRO 68)
BT 1831-May 1832, 1833-36 (no M 1836, no B) (LMA)

HANWELL St Mary, Church Road (1,213) [Elthorne Hundred; Brentford Union]
OR C 1570-1864, M 1571-1879, B 1570-1928 (LMA: DRO 6)
BT 1630, 1639 (GL); 1800-22, 1833, 1835, 1841-48, 1850-68 (no M 1841-47, 1850-68) (LMA)
Cop M 1570-1812 (Ptd, Phillimore 1, 1909); M 1630, 1639 (Ts I GL, LMA, SG, CRW); M 1570-1812 (Boyd); M 1790-1837 (Pallot Index); M 1813-35 (WMI); M 1571-1812 (I, SG)

HANWELL Independent Chapel f 1836 Boston Manor Road, later rebuilt in Westminster Road
OR no registers known

HANWORTH St George, Castle Way, Hanworth Park (671) [Spelthorne Hundred; Staines Union]
OR C 1731-1964, M 1731-1968, Banns 1823-78, 1934-60, B 1731-1927 (no M 1807-14) (LMA: DRO 18)
BT 1629-30, 1639 (GL); 1800-04, 1813-68, 1870 (no M 1837-42, 1847-70) (LMA)
Cop M 1629-30 (Ts I GL, LMA, SG, CRW); M 1732-1837 (Ptd, Phillimore 4, 1912); M 1732-1837 (Boyd); M 1790-1837 (Pallot Index); M 1732-1837 (I, SG)
Cop (Mf) C 1731-1905, M 1732-1837, B 1731-1812 (LMA)

HAREFIELD St Mary the Virgin, off Church Hill (1,285) [Elthorne Hundred; Uxbridge Union]
OR C 1538-1891, M 1546-1893, Banns 1754-1812, 1824-74, B 1538-1898 (LMA: DRO 80)
BT 1813-16, 1818-24 (LMA)
Cop M 1546-1837 (Ptd, Phillimore 5, 1914); M 1546-1837 (Boyd); M 1790-1837 (Pallot Index)

HAREFIELD Baptist Chapel f 1833
OR no registers known

HARLINGTON St Peter and St Paul (648) [Elthorne Hundred; Staines Union]
OR CMB 1540+ (Inc)
BT 1629-30, 1639 (GL); 1800-09, 1813-14, 1828-29, 1833-41, CB 1844-53 (LMA)
Cop M 1540-1812 (Ptd, Phillimore 1, 1909); C 1540-1845, M 1540-1853, B 1540-1841
  (Ptd, C. Zouch & P.T. Sherwood, 1986); M 1629-30, 1639 (Ts I GL, LMA, SG,
  CRW); CMB 1602-1812 (Essex RO); M 1540-1812 (Boyd); M 1813-37 (WMI)

HARLINGTON Baptist Chapel, High Street f 1798
OR no registers known

HARMONDSWORTH St Mary (1,276) [Elthorne Hundred; Staines Union]
OR C 1670-1958, M 1671-1979, Banns 1754-1812, 1908-43, B 1670-1900
  (LMA: DRO 123)
BT 1629-30, 1639 (GL); 1801-10, 1813-27 (LMA)
Cop CMB 1629-30, 1639, C 1670-1840, M 1671-1837, B 1670-1837
  (Ptd, West Middlesex FHS, 1991); M 1629-30, 1671-1837 (Ts I GL, LMA, SG,
  CRW); C 1670-1876, M 1671-1876 (IGI); M 1813-36 (Pallot Index); M 1813-37
  (WMI)
Cop (Mf) C 1670-1875, M 1670-1875, B 1670-1875 (LMA, SLC)

HARMONDSWORTH Meeting House, Longford (Society of Friends) (registers
  listed more fully in introduction)
OR Z 1662-1838, M 1670-72, 1764-90, 1795-1837, B 1672-1837
  (PRO: RG 6/525, 542, 547-48, 831, 838-39)
Cop Z 1662-1838, M 1670-72, 1764-90, 1795-1837, B 1672-1837 (Friends' House)

HARROW on the HILL St Mary, Church Hill (3,861) [Gore Hundred; Hendon Union]
  (Peculiar of the archbishop of Canterbury until 1845)
OR C 1562-1905, M 1559-1918, ML 1749-76, 1814-66, Banns 1653-62, 1754-1967,
  B 1558-1884 (LMA: DRO 4)
BT 1671, 1702-03, 1799, 1801-13 (LPL); 1814-27, 1829-58, 1861-67, 1869-75
  (no M 1844, 1861) (LMA)
Cop CMB 1558-1653 (Ptd, W.D. Williams, 1900-01); CMB 1653-1840 (SG);
  M 1558-1653 (Boyd)

HARROW on the HILL Independent Chapel, Hindes Road f 1659
OR no registers known

HARROW on the HILL Baptist Chapel, College Road f 1812
OR Z 1831-36 (PRO: RG 4/1239)
Cop Z 1831-36 (Ptd Mf, CRW and NMFHS, 1985)
Cop (Mf) Z 1831-36 (SLC)

HARROW on the HILL Alperton Baptist Chapel, Ealing Road f 1824
OR no registers known

HAYES St Mary (1,575) [Elthorne Hundred; Uxbridge Union] (Peculiar of the archbishop
  of Canterbury until 1845)
OR CM 1557-1942, Banns 1654-56, 1754-92, 1844-99, B 1557-1943 (LMA: DRO 47)
BT 1799-1800, 1802-03, 1805-13, 1836 (LPL); 1814-27, 1830-35, CB 1846-56 (LMA);
  1857 (LMA: DRO 47)
Cop M 1557-1813 (Ptd, Phillimore 2, 1910); CMB 1557-1840 (Ts SG);
  M 1557-1813 (Boyd); M 1790-1813 (Pallot Index); M 1814-35 (WMI)

HENDON St Mary, Church End (3,110) [Gore Hundred; Hendon Union]
OR C 1653-1992, M 1654-1989, B 1653-1953 (LMA: DRO 29)
BT 1630 (GL); 1800-09, 1811-52 (LMA)
Cop M 1630 (Ts I GL, LMA, SG, CRW); M 1653-1837 (SG); M 1754-1837 (LMA)

HENDON St Paul, The Ridgeway, Mill Hill (created from Hendon, 1833)
OR C 1836+, M 1840+, B 1842+ (Inc)

HENDON Mill Hill Chapel, Broadway (Independent)
OR ZC 1784-1830 (PRO: RG 4/377)
Cop ZC 1784-1830 (Ptd Mf, CRW and NMFHS, 1985)
Cop (Mf) ZC 1784-1830 (SLC)

HENDON Grammar School Chapel, Mill Hill (Independent) f 1808
OR ZC 1831-37 (PRO: RG 4/376)
Cop ZC 1831-37 (Ptd Mf, CRW and NMFHS, 1985)
Cop (Mf) ZC 1831-37 (SLC)

HESTON St Leonard, Heston Road (3,407) [Isleworth Hundred; Brentford Union]
OR C 1560-1965, M 1560-1946, Banns 1754-1809, B 1560-1913, Graves register
    1884-1902 (LMA: DRO 26)
BT 1639 (GL); 1800-04, 1809-10, 1813-24, 1835-36, CB 1838-45, 1847-50 (LMA)
Cop M 1559-1812 (Ptd, Phillimore 1, 1909); M 1639 (Ts I GL, LMA, SG, CRW);
    C 1703-67 (LMA); M 1813-19 (Ts SG); M 1559-1812 (Boyd); M 1790-1812 (Pallot
    Index); M 1813-37 (WMI)

HIGHGATE Cemetery, Swain's Lane
OR B 1839-1984 (with indexes) (Camden Local Studies Library, Theobalds Road)
BT B 1839-58, 1861-71 (LMA)

HIGHGATE St Michael, South Grove (chapelry in Hornsey and St Pancras until 1834)
    [Ossulstone Hundred; Edmonton Union]
OR C 1633-1952, M 1635-1753, 1832-1949, B 1633-1903 (LMA)
BT CB 1813-17, CMB 1832-33 (LMA)
Cop M 1635-1757 (Phil Ms); C 1633-1848, M 1635-1757, 1832-46, B 1633-1903
    (Ts I SG); B 1633-1903 (Index, Mf, NMFHS, 1992)

HIGHGATE Salem or New Chapel, now South Grove (Independent) f 1662
OR ZC 1785-89, 1810-36 (PRO: RG 4/1131)
Cop ZC 1785-89, 1810-36 (Ptd Mf, CRW and NMFHS, 1985)
Cop (Mf) ZC 1785-89, 1810-36 (SLC)

HIGHGATE Tabernacle, Southwood Lane (Baptist) f 1812
OR no registers known

HILLINGDON St John the Baptist, Uxbridge Road (6,885) [Elthorne Hundred;
    Uxbridge Union]
OR C 1560-1909, M 1559-1910, Banns 1768-1807, 1828-1902, B 1559-1948,
    Cemetery B 1867-1903 (LMA: DRO 110)
BT 1800-11, 1813-14, 1820-59 (no M 1829, 1838-59) (LMA)
Cop M 1559-1813 (Ptd, Phillimore 2, 1910); C 1559-1909, M 1559-1910, Banns 1845-66,
    B 1559-1948 (SG); M 1813-37 (WMI)

HOLBORN St Andrew, Holborn Viaduct (32,904) [Ossulstone Hundred; Holborn Union]
OR C 1558-1889, M 1559-1952, Banns 1754-62, 1862-93, 1900-53, B 1558-1855 (GL)
BT 1639-40, 1833-34 (GL); 1800-32 (LMA)
Cop (Mf) C 1791-1849, M 1774-1838, B 1768-1838 (LMA)

HOLBORN Ely Chapel alias St Etheldreda (chapel in the town house of the bishop of Ely; from 1874 St Etheldreda Roman Catholic church)
OR M 1709-21, 1724-34, 1738-44 (Cambridge University Library: G/I/10); C 1780-1802, M 1753-59 (Church of England Records Centre, Galleywall Road, Bermondsey)
Cop M 1705-59 (Ptd, A. Gibbons, *Ely Diocesan Records*, 1891); M 1705-59 (Boyd)

HOLBORN Trinity Chapel, Leather Lane (Independent) f 1835
OR ZC 1835-37 (PRO: RG 4/4502)

HOLBORN Providence Chapel, Grays Inn Lane (formerly in Tichfield Street, St Marylebone) (Independent)
OR ZC 1784-1835 (PRO: RG 4/4240-42)

HOLBORN Swedenborgian Church, Cross Street, Hatton Garden f 1797
OR ZC 1797-1837 (PRO: RG 4/4269, 4399)

HOLBORN Trinity Chapel, Cross Street and Leather Lane (Independent)
OR C 1813-33 (PRO: RG 4/4157)

HOLBORN Swedenborgian Church, Brownlow Street (later in Dudley Court, St Giles in the Fields
OR ZC 1805-14 (PRO: RG 4/4379)

HORNSEY St Mary, High Street (4,856) [Ossulstone Hundred; Edmonton Union]
OR C 1653-1964, M 1654-1966, ML 1754-1839, Banns 1701-07, 1754, 1823-99, 1912-61, B 1654-1892 (LMA: DRO 20)
BT 1800-52, 1854-65 (no M 1811, 1856-65) (LMA)
Cop M 1654-1837 (Ts I GL, LMA, SG, CRW); M 1654-1837 (Phil Ms)

HOUNSLOW Holy Trinity, High Street (created from Heston and Isleworth, 1836)
OR C 1708-40, 1836-99, M 1708-40, 1836-1911, Banns 1836-1940, B 1721-39, 1836-1930 (LMA: DRO 16)
BT CB 1836-50 (LMA)
Cop M 1708-53 (Ptd, Phillimore 4, 1912); M 1708-53 (Boyd); M 1836-37 (WMI); M 1708-1812 (I, SG)

HOUNSLOW Meeting House, Bell Road (Methodist) b by 1796
OR no registers known

HOUNSLOW Independent Chapel, Ship Lane f 1824
OR ZC 1827-36, B 1829-33 (PRO: RG 4/1946)
Cop ZC 1827-36, B 1829-33 (Ptd Mf, CRW and NMFHS, 1985)
Cop (Mf) ZC 1827-36, B 1829-33 (SLC)

HOUNSLOW Meeting House (Primitive Methodist) f c1833, rebuilt 1874 in Staines Road, closed in 1930s
OR no registers known

ICKENHAM St Giles, Long Lane (297) [Elthorne Hundred; Uxbridge Union]
OR C 1539-1874, M 1558-1948, Banns 1754-1814, 1823-54, 1861-1965, B 1539-1929 (LMA: DRO 27)
BT 1629-30, 1639 (GL); 1811-62 (no M 1813, 1815, 1817, 1819, 1836, 1838-57, 1862) (LMA)
Cop M 1558-1812 (Ptd, Phillimore 2, 1910); M 1813-37 (Ts I GL, LMA, SG, CRW); CB 1579-1728 (C of A); C 1813-74, M 1754-1841 (IGI); M 1558-1812 (Boyd); M 1813-37 (WMI); M 1558-1812 (I, SG)
Cop (Mf) C 1813-74 (SG)

ICKENHAM Independent Chapel, Swakeleys Road f 1831
OR records with Church Secretary

INNER TEMPLE (288) (extra-parochial) (Inn of Court)

ISLEWORTH All Saints, South Street (5,590) [Isleworth Hundred; Brentford Union]
OR C 1564-1852, M 1566-1895, B 1566-1879 (Hounslow Library Centre; many of these
    registers have been severely damaged by fire in 1942)
BT 1768 (GL); 1800-23, 1827-30 (LMA)
Cop C 1566-1852, M 1566-1895, Banns 1745-1816, B 1566-1747, 1782-1812 (Ms SG);
    M 1768 (Ts I GL, LMA, SG, CRW); B 1566-1879 (Ts SG): M 1814-37 (WMI);
    C 1813-52, M 1813-75 (IGI)
Cop (Mf) C 1556-1780, 1782-1852, M 1556-1643, 1654-1775, 1801-75, B 1556-1780,
    1782-1875 (LMA)

ISLEWORTH Our Lady of Sorrows and St Bridget, Shrewsbury Place
    (Roman Catholic) f 1675 b 1909
OR C 1746-1809, D 1766-1801 (Westminster Diocesan Archives); C 1810+, M 1838+.
    D 1858-94, B 1986+ (Inc)
Cop C 1746-1809, D 1766-1801 (Ptd, CRS 13, 1913); C 1746-1835 (IGI)

ISLEWORTH Meeting House. Conduit Lane (Quaker) b 1785
BT B 1865-97 (LMA)

ISLEWORTH Independent Chapel, North Street f 1810 b 1829 rebuilt 1914 in
    Twickenham Road
OR no registers known

ISLINGTON New Bunhill Fields Burial Ground, Church Street
OR B 1831-53 (LMA: B/NBF/1-5)

ISLINGTON St Mary, High Street (37,316) [Ossulstone Hundred; Islington Union]
    (transferred to London, 1889)
OR C 1557-1905, M 1557-1921, B 1558-1893, workhouse ZD 1839-67 (LMA)
BT 1629-30 (GL); 1800-11, 1813 (LMA)
Cop M 1629-30 (Ts I GL, LMA, SG, CRW); C 1831-36, M 1784-1812 (Ts I only SG);
    C 1752-1837, M 1751-1837 (Ts I only, SG)

ISLINGTON Holy Trinity, Cloudesley Square (created from Islington St Mary, 1830)
    (transferred to London, 1889)
OR C 1829-1978, M 1830-1977, B 1829-54 (LMA)
Cop M 1830-37 (Ts CRW, LMA, SG); C 1829-37, B 1829-54 (I, SG)

ISLINGTON St John the Evangelist, Pemberton Gardens, Upper Holloway (created from
    Islington St Mary, 1830) (transferred to London, 1889)
OR C 1830-1954, M 1830-1952, B 1829-54 (LMA)
Cop B 1829-54 (Ts SG); C 1830-37, M 1830-37, B 1829-54 (Ts I only, SG)

ISLINGTON St Paul, Essex Road, Ball's Pond, Canonbury (created from Islington
    St Mary, 1830) (transferred to London, 1889)
OR C 1830-1980, M 1831-1954 (LMA)
BT 1830-45 (no M 1837-45, no B) (LMA)
Cop C 1830-38, M 1831-37 (Ts I only, SG)

ISLINGTON Independent Chapel, New Court, Tollington Park f 1662
OR no registers known

ISLINGTON St Anne, Meeting House Court (Presbyterian) f 1671 b 1692 moved to Little Carter Lane, Blackfriars, 1721 and Upper Street, 1734
OR C 1711-57, 1760-1811 (PRO: RG 4/4141, 4231)
Cop C 1711-1811 (IGI)

ISLINGTON Lower Street Chapel (Independent) f 1730
OR ZC 1769-1837 (PRO: RG 4/4191)

ISLINGTON Independent Chapel, Upper Street f 1788 (burial ground also known as New Bunhill Fields)
OR ZC 1804-37 (PRO: RG 4/4190, 4342); B 1831-53 (LMA: B/NBF)

ISLINGTON Union Chapel, Compton Terrace (Independent) f 1804
OR ZC 1805-37 (PRO: RG 4/4189)

ISLINGTON Independent Chapel, Camden Road, Caledonian Road, Holloway f 1804
OR ZC 1815-37 (PRO: RG 4/4309)

ISLINGTON Salter's Hall, Baxter Road, Canonbury (Baptist) f 1821
OR no registers known

ISLINGTON Maberley Chapel, Balls Pond Road (Independent) f 1825
OR ZC 1826-37 (PRO: RG 4/4270)

ISLINGTON Wesleyan Chapel, Liverpool Road f 1828
OR ZC 1828-37 (PRO: RG 4/4271)
Cop ZC 1828-37 (Ts GL, SG)

ISLINGTON Scotch Church, River Terrace formerly Chadwell Street f 1828
OR ZC 1829-39 (PRO: RG 4/4272)

ISLINGTON Irvingite Church, Duncan Street, Islington Green f 1834
OR ZC 1834-40 (PRO: RG 4/4531)

ISLINGTON Barnsbury Chapel (Independent) f 1835
OR ZC 1835-37 (PRO: RG 4/4341)

KENSAL GREEN *see* **WILLESDEN**

KENSINGTON St Mary Abbots (20,902) [Ossulstone Hundred; Kensington Union] (transferred to London, 1889)
OR CM 1539+, B 1539-1853 (Inc)
BT 1639 (GL); 1800-45 (no M 1820-45) (LMA)
Cop CB 1539-1676, M 1539-1675 (Ptd, HS 16, 1890); M 1676-1775 (Ptd, B.R. Curle, 1969); CM 1676-1701, B 1676-92 (LMA, Kensington Lib); C 1675-1850, M 1775-1837, B 1675-1853 (Ts I SG); M 1639 (Ts I GL, LMA, SG, CRW)(SG)

KENSINGTON Holy Trinity Brompton Road (created from Kensington St Mary Abbots, 1830) (transferred to London, 1889)
OR C 1829-1981, M 1830-1987, B 1829-1916 (LMA)
BT C 1888-90 (LMA)
Cop C 1829-34 (Ts, I only, SG); B 1829-45 (Ts I SG)

KENSINGTON Essex Street, Strand (Presbyterian) f 1774 moved to Palace Gardens Terrace, 1887
OR C 1814-27 (PRO: RG 4/4488)

KENSINGTON St Mary later (1869) Our Lady of Victories, Holland Street
(Roman Catholic) f 1812 (Cath Dir 1965)
OR C 1811-13, 1828+, M 1852+ (Inc)

KENSINGTON Hornton Street Chapel (Independent) f 1793
OR ZC 1825-37 (PRO: RG 4/1947)
Cop ZC 1825-37 (Ptd Mf, CRW and NMFHS, 1985)
Cop (Mf) ZC 1825-37 (SLC)

KENSINGTON Trevor Chapel, Brompton Row, Arthur Street (Independent)
OR ZC 1816-37 (PRO: RG 4/4378)

KINGSBURY St Andrew later Holy Innocents, Kingsbury Road (463) [Gore Hundred;
Hendon Union]
OR C 1732-1913, M 1735-1837, Banns 1769-1910, B 1732-1878 (LMA: DRO 45)
BT 1639 (GL); 1800-09, 1812-13, 1816, 1833-73 (no M 1838-73) (LMA)
Cop M 1639 (Ts I GL, LMA, SG, CRW)

KNIGHTSBRIDGE *see* **ST MARGARET WESTMINSTER**

LALEHAM All Saints, Laleham Village (588) [Spelthorne Hundred; Staines Union]
(chapelry in Staines until 1859) (transferred to Surrey 1965)
OR C 1538-1692, 1789-1801, 1804-1915, M 1539-1683, 1754-1937, Banns 1885-1911,
1919-22, B 1538-1690, 1789-1802, 1804-89 (LMA: DRO 21); CMB 1696-1710 (LMA:
DRO 78)
BT 1630, 1639 (GL); 1800-07, 1812-45, 1847-57 (no M 1820, 1825-26, 1832, 1834,
1839-40, 1844, 1847-57), M 1824 in Ashford BT for that year (LMA)
Cop C 1538-1692, 1789-1839, M 1539-1683, 1754-1838, B 1538-1690, 1789-1842
(Ts SG); M 1630, 1639 (Ts I GL, LMA, SG, CRW); M 1813-37 (WMI)

LIMEHOUSE St Anne, Commercial Road (15,695) [Ossulstone Hundred; Stepney Union]
(created from Stepney, 1725) (transferred to London, 1889)
OR C 1730-1955, M 1730-1968, B 1730-1897 (LMA)
BT 1800-37 (LMA)
Cop M 1754-71 (Ts I only, SG)

LIMEHOUSE Brunswick Chapel, Three Colt Street (Wesleyan Methodist) f 1831
OR ZCB 1831-37 (PRO: RG 4/4277, 4247); C 1909-63, M 1900-54, B 1831-53
(LMA: N/M/42)

LINCOLN'S INN Chapel (142 the extra-parochial part) (part extra-parochial place)
[Ossulstone Hundred; not in Union] (transferred to London, 1889)
OR C 1716+, M 1695-1754, 1840+, B 1695-1852 (Lincoln's Inn Library)
Cop C 1716-1806, M 1695-1754, B 1695-1852 (Ptd, anon, *The records of the
Honourable Society of Lincoln's Inn* 2, 1896); M 1695-1754 (Boyd); C 1716-49, 1774,
1786-1806 (IGI)

**LINCOLN'S INN FIELDS Sardinian Embassy Chapel, Duke Street later (1860) St Anselm
and St Cecilia** reb 1909 in Kingsway (Roman Catholic) f 1687 (Cath Dir 1965)
OR C 1731+, M 1729+ (Inc)
Cop C 1731-72, M 1729-1831 (Ptd, CRS 19, 1917); M 1856-70 (I Institute of Heraldic &
Genealogical Studies, Canterbury)

LINCOLN'S INN Gate Street Chapel (Lady Huntingdon's Connexion) f 1792
OR ZC 1827-37 (PRO: RG 4/4193); Z 1791-1817 (PRO: RG 8/67)

LITTLETON St Mary Magdalen (134) [Spelthorne Hundred; Staines Union] (transferred to Surrey 1965)
OR C 1579-1652, 1664-1981, M 1564-1637, 1664-1984, B 1562-1637, 1664-1962 (LMA: DRO 128)
BT 1629-30, 1639 (GL); 1812-14, 1819, 1824, 1827, 1833, 1838-52 (no M 1812, 1814, 1827, 1838-52) (LMA)
Cop C 1579-1852, M 1564-1810, B 1562-1851 (Ts I SG); C 1579-1812, M 1564-1751, B 1562-1812 (Ts GL); M 1629-30, 1639 (Ts I GL, LMA, SG, CRW); M 1813-35 (SG); M 1813, 1819, 1833 (WMI); C 1579-1679, 1699-1812, M 1564-1652, 1664-1751 (IGI)

LONDON Dissenters General Register (kept by various ministers)
OR Z 1728-96 (PRO: RG 4/4403)

LONDON and MIDDLESEX Quarterly Meeting (Society of Friends) (registers listed more fully in introduction)
OR Z 1646-1837, M 1658-1836, M certificates 1670-1719, B 1661-1837 (PRO: RG 6)
Cop Z 1646-1837, M 1658-1836, M certificates 1670-1719, B 1661-1837 (Friends' House)

LYON'S INN f 1420 no register kept

MIDDLE TEMPLE (195) (extra-parochial) (Inn of Court) *see* **TEMPLE** in City section

MILL HILL *see* **HENDON**

MIMMS, SOUTH St Giles (2,010) [part Edmonton Hundred, Middlesex, part Cashio Hundred, Hertfordshire; Barnet Union] (original Hertfordshire part transferred to Monken Hadley, 1894, the whole remaining parish transferred to Hertfordshire, 1965)
OR C 1558-1856, M 1558-1906, ML 1776-1839, Banns 1823-92, B 1558-1898 (LMA: DRO 5)
BT 1800-11, 1813-23, 1840 (no CB 1823) (LMA)
Cop (Mf) B 1900-83 (SG)

MIMMS, SOUTH St John the Baptist, later St Mary the Virgin and All Saints, Potters Bar (created from South Mimms, 1835)
OR C 1835-70, B 1835-92 (Herts Archives); M 1840+ (Inc)
BT 1835-86 (no M 1835-39, 1842) (LMA)

MIMMS, SOUTH Meeting House, Hampstead End, Winchmore Hill (Society of Friends) (registers listed more fully in introduction)
OR Z 1651-1726, M 1675-1726, B 1666-1726 (PRO: RG 6/506, 543, 549-50, 840, 848, 1177, 1297)
Cop Z 1651-1726, M 1675-1726, B 1666-1726 (Friends' House)

MIMMS, SOUTH Baptist Chapel, Barnet Road, Potters Bar f 1788
OR no registers known

MINORIES, HOLY TRINITY IN THE (508) [Ossulstone Hundred; Whitechapel Union] (transferred to London, 1889) (priory church in St Botolph Aldgate, Middlesex, created a parish, 1557)
OR C 1563-1897, M 1580-1898, Banns 1754-1898, B 1566-1852 (GL)
BT 1629-30, 1638-39, 1810-48 (no M 1838-48) (GL); CB 1843, 1845 (LMA)
Cop M 1644-48, 1657-83 (Ms GL); C 1563-1875 (IGI); M 1579-1663 (Boyd); M 1799-1837 (Pallot Index); B 1813-52 (CLBI); M 1676-92 (Mf, ELFHS, 1988-92)

NEW INN (extra-parochial) (Inn of Court) f 1485

NORTHOLT St Mary, Ealing Road (447) [Elthorne Hundred; Uxbridge Union]
OR C 1560-1942, M 1575-1949, Banns 1754-1812, 1824-1944, B 1583-1942
    (LMA: DRO 51)
BT 1639 (GL); 1801-02, Apr 1805-May 1806, 1807-08, 1810, 1812, 1822-33, 1835,
    1838-41 (LMA); 1842-43 and 1844-45 (LMA: DRO 51; never submitted)
Cop M 1575-1812 (Ptd, Phillimore 2, 1910); M 1639 (Ts I GL, LMA, SG, CRW);
    CMB 1560-1812, Banns 1754-1812 (Westminster Abbey Muniment Room);
CB 1700-1812, M 1575-1812 (Ts SG)

NORTON FOLGATE (1,918) (extra-parochial liberty; probably at one time part of
    St Botolph Bishopsgate outside the City) [Ossulstone Hundred; Whitechapel Union]
    (transferred to London, 1889)

NORTON FOLGATE Sir George Wheeler's Chapel, later St Mary Spital Square
OR C 1733-1911, M 1720-52, 1845-1911 (LMA)
Cop M 1720-52 (Ptd, *Collectanea Topographica et Genealogica* 3, pp.381-389, 1836);
    M 1720-52 (GL: Challen 39, SG); C 1733-1841 (Ts I SG); M 1720-52 (Boyd); C 1733-
    1876, M 1720-52, 1845-85 (IGI)

NORWOOD St Mary the Virgin, Tentelow Road (1,320) [Elthorne Hundred;
    Uxbridge Union] (chapelry in Hayes until 1725) (Peculiar of the archbishop of
    Canterbury until 1845)
OR C 1654-1962, M 1654-1970, Banns 1754-83,1824-66, B 1654-1883 (LMA: DRO 25)
BT 1671-74, 1799, 1808, 1810-12 (LPL); 1813-15, 1858 (LMA)
Cop M 1654-1837 (Ts I GL, LMA, SG, CRW); M 1813-37 (WMI)

OLD ARTILLERY GROUND (1,411) (Liberty) [Ossulstone Hundred; Whitechapel Union]
    (transferred to London, 1889)

OLD ARTILLERY GROUND Parliament Court, Bishopsgate (Irvingite) f 1824
OR C 1829-40 (PRO: RG 4/4375)
Cop C 1829-40 (SG); C 1829-40 (IGI)

PADDINGTON Queen's Lying-in Hospital, Cambridge Place
OR Z 1791-97 (St Marylebone Library)

PADDINGTON St James, Sussex Gardens (14,500) [Ossulstone Hundred; Paddington
    Union] (transferred to London, 1889) b 1843 and became parish church in 1845, the
    old St Mary Paddington becoming a chapelry
OR C 1655-1950, M 1656-1958, B 1655-1896 (B 1790-1896 classified under St Mary
    Paddington) (LMA)
BT 1630 (GL); 1832-42 (no M 1832-35, 1838-42) (St James); 1803-49 (no M 1838-49)
    (St Mary) (LMA)
Cop M 1630 (Ts I GL, LMA, SG, CRW), M 1784-92 (SG); M 1818-37 (Paddington
    Lib); M 1754-1837, B 1813-40 (Ts I only, SG)

PADDINGTON St John the Evangelist, Hyde Park Gate
OR C 1832-1939, M 1832-1944, B 1833-54 (LMA); C 1939+, M 1944+ (Inc)
BT 1832-42 (no M 1838-42, no B 1832) (LMA)
Cop B 1833-54 (Ts I SG)

PADDINGTON St Sophia's Cathedral, Moscow Road, Bayswater (Greek Orthodox)
    f 1676 b 1879

PADDINGTON French Church, Paddington Green f 1802
OR CM 1798 (Archives de Nantes)

PADDINGTON Paddington Chapel, New Road (Independent) f 1813
OR ZC 1813-36 (PRO: RG 4/4348)

PADDINGTON Irvingite Church, Harrow Road f 1835
OR C 1835-40 (PRO: RG 4/4337)

PADDINGTON Baptist Chapel, Porchester Road, Westbourne Park f 1836
OR no registers known

PERIVALE St Mary the Virgin with St Nicholas, Perivale Lane (sometimes known as
   Little Greenford or Greenford Parva) (32) [Elthorne Hundred; Brentford Union]
OR C 1707-1956, M 1720-1968, Banns 1950-84, B 1720-1988, register of graves
   1862-1945 (LMA: DRO 73)
BT 1639 (GL); 1800-08, 1811-12, 1833-38 (no M 1811-12, 1833-35, 1838, no B 1837-38)
   (LMA)
Cop M 1629-30, 1639 (Ts I GL, LMA, SG, CRW); C 1707-1855, M 1720-1844,
   B 1720-1952 (Ts GL, SG); D 1862-1907 (SG)

PINNER St John the Baptist, Church Lane (1,270) [Gore Hundred; Hendon Union]
   (chapelry in Harrow until 1766) (Peculiar of the archbishop of Canterbury until 1845)
OR C 1654-1934, M 1655-1942, Banns 1950-60, ML 1887,1960, B 1654-1861 (and a few
   to 1933) (LMA: DRO 8)
BT 1799, 1801-06, 1808-12 (LPL); 1813-27, 1829, 1831-35, 1846-68, 1873, 1875
   (no M 1853-75) (LMA); 1828 (LMA: DRO 8; never submitted)
Cop M 1654-1837 (Ptd, Phillimore 4, 1912); C 1645-1812, M 1655-1931, B 1654-78,
   1813-61 (LMA); 1654-1837 (Boyd); M 1813-37 (WMI); M 1790-1837 (Pallot Index)

POPLAR Workhouse, Poplar High Street
OR Z 1837-1914, C 1881-1939, D 1860-1931 (LMA)
Cop Z 1837-75 (IGI)
Cop (Mf) Z 1837-75 (SLC, LMA)

POPLAR All Saints, East India Dock Road (16,849) [Ossulstone Hundred; Poplar Union]
   transferred to London, 1889) (originally what is now St Matthias, Woodstock Terrace,
   East India Company chapel, chapelry of Stepney from 1654, new church and separate
   parish, 1817, old chapel remained in use, but registers went to All Saints)
OR C 1728-33,1775-76,1788-1922, M 1711-54,1823-1949, B 1802-46 (LMA);
   B 1825-55 (Tower Hamlets Library)
BT 1813-89 (no M 1813-22, 1843-89, no B 1866, 1869, 1871-72, 1874-89) (LMA)
Cop M 1711-54 (GL: Challen 52); C 1728-33, 1775-76, 1802-12 (SG);
   B 1654-1812 (Tower Hamlets Lib); C 1728-33, 1775-76, 1802-37, M 1711-54,
   1823-37, B 1825-55 (LMA); M 1823-37 (SG); B 1824-38 (Ptd ESFHS, Mf 1991)

POPLAR Wesleyan Chapel, Hale Street f 1780
OR ZC 1812-37 (PRO: RG 4/4310)

POPLAR Union Chapel, Bow Lane (Independent) f 1812
OR ZC 1812-37 (PRO: RG 4/4166)

POPLAR St Mary and St Joseph, Canton Street (Roman Catholic) f 1816
   (Cath Dir 1965) (New Chapel, Wade Street in Cath Dir 1828)
OR CM 1818+ (Inc)
Cop M 1856-70 (I Institute of Heraldic & Genealogical Studies, Canterbury)

POPLAR Mill Wall Chapel (Independent) f 1817
OR ZC 1823-36 (PRO: RG 4/4167)

POPLAR Central Hall, Bruce Street (Methodist)
OR C 1833-1940 (LMA: acc.1850/249-50)

PORTPOOL Liberty (in St Andrew Holborn and Gray's Inn)

POTTERS BAR *see* **MIMMS, SOUTH**

ROLLS, Liberty of the, Rolls Chapel, Chancery Lane (2,682) [Ossulstone Hundred;
Holborn Union] (originally a house with a chapel for converted Jews, until 17th
century, used for storing Chancery records until the erection of the Public Record
Office on the site 1856-70; transferred to London, 1889; chapel demolished, 1895)
OR C 1837, 1860-92, M 1736-49, 1845-85, ML 1744-46, B 1738-1826
(PRO: PRO 30/21/3/1; PRO 30/21/3/2-4)
Cop M 1736-49, B 1738-1826 (Ptd, *57th Report of the Deputy Keeper of the Public
Records, Parl.Papers* 1896, vol.48); M 1736-49, 1751 (Ptd, *Collectanea topographica
et genealogica* 3, 1836); M 1736-49 (Boyd); C 1842-75, M 1845-85 (IGI)

RUISLIP St Martin, High Street (1,197) [Elthorne Hundred; Uxbridge Union]
OR C 1689-1757, 1761-1949, M 1694-1717, 1744-1949, Banns 1795-1823, 1858-1911,
1952-71, B 1695-1957, Registers of graves 1906-38, (LMA: DRO 19)
BT 1629-30 (GL); 1800-34, 1840, 1854-58 (no M 1854-58) (LMA)
Cop C 1685-1840, M 1694-1840, B 1695-1840 (SG); M 1629-30 (Ts I GL, LMA, SG,
CRW); M 1813-37 (WMI)

SAFFRON HILL, HATTON GARDEN and ELY RENTS, Liberty of (9,745) [Ossulstone
Hundred; Holborn Union] (adjacent to St Andrew Holborn; transferred to London,
1889)

ST BOTOLPH WITHOUT ALDGATE, Aldgate High Street (13,068) (part City of
London, part Middlesex (East Smithfield Liberty) [Ossulstone Hundred; Whitechapel
Union] (transferred to London, 1889) (united with Holy Trinity in the Minories, 1893)
OR C 1558-1927, M 1558-1945, Banns 1754-1878, B 1558-1853 (GL)
BT 1802-15 (no CB 1815) (GL)
Cop CMB 1593-1640 (Ms I only GL); C 1558-1875 (IGI); B 1813-53 (CLBI 3)

ST CLEMENT DANES, Westminster (15,442) [part Ossulstone Hundred, part City of
Westminster; Strand Union] (transferred to London, 1889)
OR C 1558-1948, M 1558-1940, Banns 1754-90, 1810-26, 1843-80, 1920-22, 1929-42,
B 1558-1853 (WPL)
BT 1807-27, 1843-53 (no M 1843-53) (LMA)

ST CLEMENT DANES Independent Chapel, Carey Street, New Court f 1687
OR Z 1786-1837, C 1707-1837 (PRO: RG 4/4228-30, 4484)

ST CLEMENT DANES Presbyterian Church, Essex Street, Strand f 1774
OR C 1814-27, B 1814-22 (PRO: RG 4/4488)

ST GEORGE HANOVER SQUARE, Westminster, George Street (58,209) [City of
Westminster; St George Hanover Square Union] (transferred to London, 1889) (created
from St Martin in the Fields, 1724)
OR C 1725-1914 (also C 1866-92 in workhouse, C 1879-1900 in Union), M 1725-1895,
Banns 1789-92, 1833-38, 1872-76, B 1725-1874 (WPL)
BT 1800-32 (LMA)
Cop M 1725-87 (Ptd, HS 11, 1886); M 1788-1809 (Ptd, HS 14, 1888); M 1810-23
(Ptd, HS 22, 1896); M 1824-37 (Ptd, HS 24, 1897); M 1837-45 (Ms I M by licence
only SG); M 1725-1837 (Boyd)

ST GEORGE HANOVER SQUARE St Mark, North Audley Street
OR M 1863-1937, Banns 1894-1951, B 1828-52 (WPL)

ST GEORGE HANOVER SQUARE St Peter, Palace Street
OR C 1822-31, 1890-1921 (WPL)

ST GEORGE HANOVER SQUARE St Peter, Eaton Square (created from St George
   Hanover Square, 1830)
OR C 1831-1965, M 1844-1989 (WPL)

ST GEORGE HANOVER SQUARE Eaton Chapel
OR C 1836-1901 (WPL)

ST GEORGE HANOVER SQUARE Grosvenor Chapel, South Audley Street
OR C 1836-75 (WPL)

**ST GEORGE HANOVER SQUARE Portuguese Embassy Chapel later Our Lady of
   Assumption and St Gregory**, South Audley Street (Roman Catholic) f 1663 in St James
   Palace, from 1671 in Somerset House, from c1700 at Portuguese Embassy, *see*
   St James Westminster, St James Palace

ST GEORGE HANOVER SQUARE St George's Chapel, Mayfair
OR C 1740-53, M 1735-54 (WPL)
Cop C 1740-53, M 1735-54 (Ptd, HS 15, 1889)

ST GEORGE HANOVER SQUARE Neapolitan Embassy Chapel, Stanhope Street
   (Roman Catholic)
OR C 1764-1855, B 1820 (Westminster Diocesan Archives)
Cop C 1764-1855, B 1820 (Ts I SG)

ST GEORGE HANOVER SQUARE Buckingham Chapel, Palace Street, Pimlico
   (Independent) f 1794
OR ZC 1795-1804, 1820-37, B 1794-1804, 1819-46 (PRO: RG 4/4253-54, 4351-52)

ST GEORGE HANOVER SQUARE Ebenezer Chapel, Mayfair (Independent)
OR ZC 1804-27, 1830-37 (PRO: RG 4/4279, 4347)

ST GEORGE HANOVER SQUARE Independent Chapel, Robert Street,
   Grosvenor Square f 1824
OR C 1827-36 (PRO: RG 4/4169)

**ST GEORGE HANOVER SQUARE French Embassy Chapel later (1853) The
   Annunciation**, Albert Gate House (Roman Catholic)
OR C 1795-1841, M 1795-1846 (Archives de Nantes); C 1842-1910, M 1846-1910
   (Westminster Diocesan Archives)
Cop C 1842-1910, M 1846-1910 (Catholic FHS); M 1846-70 (I Institute of Heraldic &
   Genealogical Studies, Canterbury)

ST GEORGE HANOVER SQUARE The Immaculate Conception, Farm Street, Hill Street,
   Berkeley Square (Roman Catholic)
OR C 1836-1966 (Inc)

ST GEORGE IN THE EAST Workhouse, Raine Street
OR Z 1836-75, D 1836-1918 (LMA)
Cop Z 1836-75 (IGI)
Cop (Mf) Z 1836-75, D 1836-75 (SLC)

ST GEORGE IN THE EAST, Cannon Street Road (38,505) [Ossulstone Hundred; St George in the East Union] (transferred to London, 1889) (created from Stepney, 1729)
OR C 1729-1901, M 1729-1894, B 1729-1875 (LMA)
BT 1805-48 (LMA)
Cop C 1836-37, B 1760-64 (SG); M 1737-95 (Ts I only SG); C 1771-1837, M 1729-1837, B 1760-73 (Ts I only, SG)
Cop (Mf) ZC 1729-79 (SG)

ST GEORGE IN THE EAST Beulah Chapel, Commercial Road (formerly at Church Lane, Whitechapel, later moved to Cameron Road, Seven Kings) f 1653
OR Z 1787-1837 (PRO: RG 4/4268)

ST GEORGE IN THE EAST Pell Street (late Nightingale Lane) (united with Old Gravel Lane) (Independent) f 1662
OR ZC 1784-1837 (PRO: RG 4/4251)

ST GEORGE IN THE EAST Old Gravel Lane (Independent) f 1704
OR ZC 1704-1837, B 1737-1837 (PRO: RG 4/4155-56, 4304)

ST GEORGE IN THE EAST Scotch Church, Broad Street (moved to St Vincent Street, Mile End Old Town, 1823)
OR ZC 1741-1840 (PRO: RG 4/4324-25)

ST GEORGE IN THE EAST Mulberry Gardens Chapel, Pell Street (Lady Huntingdon's Connexion)
OR ZC 1784-1837 (PRO: RG 4/4165)

ST GEORGE IN THE EAST Independent Chapel, Watney Street (later united with Coverdale and Ebenezer Chapels) f 1785
OR no registers known

ST GEORGE IN THE EAST Virginia Street, Ratcliff Highway (Roman Catholic) (Cath Dir 1828)

ST GEORGE IN THE EAST Wycliffe Chapel, Commercial Road, Philpot Street (formerly in Cannon Street Road) (Independent)
OR ZC 1785-1837, B 1784-1837 (PRO: RG 4/4146-53, 4182, 4295-4300, 4496); C 1792-1810, 1850-1906, M 1850-73, B 1831-40 (LMA: N/C/40)

ST GEORGE IN THE EAST Tonbridge Chapel, New Road (Independent) f 1810, *fl. c*1850, now closed
OR ZC 1811-37 (PRO: RG 4/4534)

ST GEORGE IN THE EAST St George's Chapel, New Road (Wesleyan Methodist) f 1812
OR ZC 1812-37, B 1828-54 (PRO: RG 4/4211-12, 4354)

ST GEORGE THE MARTYR, Queen Square (incl.in St Andrew Holborn population figure) [Ossulstone Hundred; Holborn Union] (transferred to London, 1889) (created from St Andrew Holborn, 1723)
OR C 1710-1955, M 1706-1950, B 1715-1855 (LMA)
BT 1800-Apr 1803, Mar 1804-31 (LMA)
Cop C 1710-40, M 1706-72 (Ptd, Parish Register Society Extra Vol. 84, 1922); C 1710-1897, M 1709-1897, B 1706-1897 (Ptd in Parish Magazines); C 1710-69, M 1709-1800, B 1714-19 (Newspaper cuttings at SG); M 1706-1801 (Boyd)

ST GEORGE THE MARTYR Eagle Street, Red Lion Square (Baptist) f 1737
OR Z 1770-1813 (PRO: RG 4/4235)

ST GILES IN THE FIELDS British Lying-in Hospital, Endell Street
OR ZC 1749-1830, Particulars 1749-1868 (PRO: RG 8/52-66)
Cop C 1749-1830 (IGI)

ST GILES IN THE FIELDS (36,432) [Ossulstone Hundred; St Giles Union] (transferred
to London, 1889)
OR CM 1561+, B 1561-1853 (Inc)
BT 1800-57, 1859-60 (no M 1838-60, no B 1859-60) (LMA)
Cop M 1561-1650 (GL: Challen 10; SG); Extr CMB 1567-1754 (Ptd, *The Genealogist* 2,
1878, pp.383-385); Extr (C of A: Chester Ms 4, pp.1-206); M 1561-1650 (Boyd)

ST GILES IN THE FIELDS West Street Chapel, Seven Dials (French Protestant)
OR C 1693-1743, M 1693-1743 (PRO: RG 4/4551)
Cop C 1693-1743, M 1693-1743 (Ptd, Hug Soc 32, 1929); C 1693-1743 (IGI);
M 1693-1743 (Boyd)

ST GILES IN THE FIELDS Baptist Chapel, Keppel Street, Russell Square f 1713
OR Z 1788-1837 (PRO: RG 4/4275)

ST GILES IN THE FIELDS Wesleyan Chapel, Great Queen Street, Lincolns Inn Fields
f 1792
OR ZC 1812-37, B 1828-36 (PRO: RG 4/4305-06); C 1812-1909, M 1843-1930,
B 1828-56 (LMA: N/M/7)

ST GILES IN THE FIELDS Swedenborgian Church, Dudley Court (formerly at
Brownlow Street, Holborn)
OR ZC 1805-14 (PRO: RG 4/4379)

ST JAMES PALACE Dutch Chapel Royal
OR C 1685-1775, M 1689-1754 (PRO: RG 4/4574-75)
Cop C 1685-1775, M 1689-1754 (Ptd, F.G.L.O. Van Kretschar, 1964);
C 1694-1775, M 1692-1754, B 1689-1774 (SG)

ST JAMES PICCADILLY, Westminster (37,053) [City of Westminster; St James parish
1762-1868, Westminster Union from 1868] (transferred to London, 1889) (created from
St Martin in the Fields, 1685)
OR C 1685-1963, M 1685-1957, Banns 1856-1932, B 1685-1853 (WPL)
BT 1800-33 (no CB 1812) (LMA)
Cop M 1685-1754 (Ms GL, C of A); M 1701-54 (Boyd); B 1754-62 (Ms GL, SG);
B 1789-1853 at St James Hampstead Road (Ts I SG)

ST JAMES PICCADILLY King's Weigh House Church, Duke Street, Grosvenor Square
see St Leonard Eastcheap in City section (Independent) f 1690s

ST JAMES PICCADILLY Glasshouse Street, Golden Square and Leicester Fields Chapel
(French Church) f 1687 in Glasshouse Street, moved to Orange Street, Leicester Fields
in 1692, closed 1786 and merged with L'Eglise du Quarre
OR C 1688-1783, M 1688-1752 (PRO: RG 4/4581-85)
Cop C 1688-1783, M 1688-1752 (Ptd, Hug Soc 29, 1926); C 1688-1783 (IGI);
M 1688-1752 (Boyd)

ST JAMES PICCADILLY Swallow Street French Church, Piccadilly
OR C 1690-1709, M 1690-1709 (PRO: RG 4/4609)
Cop C 1690-1709, M 1690-1709 (Ptd, Hug Soc 28, 1924)

ST JAMES PICCADILLY French Chapel Royal (French Church)
OR C 1700-56, M 1700-53 (PRO: RG 4/4539-41, 4640)
Cop C 1700-56, M 1700-53 (Ptd, Hug Soc 28, 1924); M 1700-54 (Boyd)

ST JAMES PICCADILLY Scotch Church, Swallow Street f 1709
OR ZC 1750-1840 (PRO: RG 4/4175, 4538)

ST JAMES PICCADILLY German Lutheran Royal Chapel, St James's Palace
OR C 1712-1836, M 1712-53 (PRO: RG 4/4568-69)

ST JAMES PICCADILLY Imperial (Austrian) Embassy Chapel, St James Square. Moved
  to Twickenham, 1784 (Roman Catholic)
OR C 1764-1820, M 1765-1820, D 1793-1807 (Westminster Diocesan Archives)
Cop C 1764-1820, M 1765-1820, D 1793-1807 (Ts I SG)

**ST JAMES PICCADILLY Bavarian Chapel, later Our Lady of the Assumption and
  St Gregory**, Warwick Street (from 1736), Golden Square. Embassy and chapel closed
  1871, when became ordinary church (Roman Catholic)
OR C 1748-1909, M 1747-1922 (Westminster Diocesan Archives); C 1909+, M 1922+,
  D 1858-65, 1930, 1958+ (Inc)
Cop C 1748-1838, M 1747-1840 (SG, Catholic FHS); M 1838-70 (I Institute of
  Heraldic & Genealogical Studies, Canterbury)
Cop (Mf) C 1748-1827, M 1747-54 (SLC)

ST JAMES PICCADILLY Chapel Royal later Portuguese Embassy Chapel
  (Roman Catholic) (extra-parochial) (from 1662 the Chapel Royal was in St James
  Palace, from 1671 in Somerset House and from 1696 as the Portuguese Chapel, which
  was in Warwick Street until 1736 (which became the Bavarian Embassy), then South
  Audley Street. closed 1828)
OR C 1663-1701, 1721-1844, M 1662-1829 (Portuguese Embassy)
Cop C 1663-1829 (Ts I SG); M 1662-1849 (Ptd, CRS 38, 1941)

ST JAMES PICCADILLY Eschol Chapel, Marshall Street later Titchfield Street,
  St Marylebone (Independent Calvinist)
OR C 1815-47 (PRO: RG 4/4355)

ST JAMES PICCADILLY Craven Chapel, Marshall Street, Regent Street (Independent)
  f 1822
OR C 1823-37 (PRO: RG 4/4194)

ST JOHN THE EVANGELIST, Westminster Millbank Penitentiary
OR C 1816-71, B 1817-53, D 1848-63 (PRO: PCOM 2/139-140,165)
Cop(Mf) C 1816-71 (SG)

ST JOHN THE EVANGELIST, Westminster (22,648) [City of Westminster; St Margaret
  and St John Union 1765-1867, St George Hanover Square Union 1867-89] (transferred
  to London, 1889) (created from St Margaret Westminster, 1727)
OR C 1729-1941, M 1728-1823, 1833-1947, Banns 1754-61, 1849-52, 1860-67,
  B 1731-1855 (WPL)
BT 1813-40, 1842 (no M 1839-42) (LMA)
Cop C 1728-55, M 1728-54, B 1731-54 (Ms GL)

ST JOHN THE EVANGELIST, St Mary Tothill Fields, Westminster (created from St John the Evangelist, Westminster, 1837)
OR C 1837-1923, M 1841-1923 (WPL)

ST JOHN THE EVANGELIST, Westminster Baptist Chapel, Horseferry Road f 1807
OR no registers known

ST JOHN THE EVANGELIST Westminster Chapel, Romney Terrace (Wesleyan Methodist) f 1815
OR ZC 1812-37 (PRO: RG 4/4313)

ST JOHN THE EVANGELIST, Westminster, St Mary Romney Terrace, Marsham Street (Roman Catholic) f 1809, closed 1903
OR C 1809+, M 1851+ (Westminster Cathedral)
Cop C 1809-38 (SG)

ST JOHN THE EVANGELIST, Westminster Irvingite Church, Rochester Row f 1835
OR ZC 1835-40 (PRO: RG 4/4170)

ST KATHARINE BY THE TOWER (72) (extra-parochial precinct; most of area flooded to create dock, 1825) [Ossulstone Hundred; Whitechapel Union] (transferred to London, 1889)
OR C 1584-1946, M 1584-1924, Banns 1754-1825, B 1584-1854 (GL)
BT none
Cop CMB 1584-1626 (Ptd, HS 75, 1945); CMB 1626-66 (Ptd, HS 76, 1946); CMB 1666-87 (Ptd, HS 77, 1947); M 1686-1726 (Ptd, HS 78-79, 1949); C 1666-95, B 1666-95 (Ptd, HS 80-81, 1952); M 1704-13 (GL: Ts Challen 52); B 1804-12 (I SG)

ST KATHARINE BY THE TOWER French Church *fl.* temp. Elizabeth
OR no registers known

ST LUKE OLD STREET Finsbury Lying-in Hospital, City Road later Hanley Road
OR C 1813-1978 (LMA: H10/CLM)
BT C 1813-31, 1833, 1835-37 (LMA: under City of London Lying-in Hospital)
Cop C 1813-40 (CD Rom, SG)

ST LUKE OLD STREET Bunhill Fields Burial Ground, City Road, Finsbury (opened 1665, closed 1854; the chief burial place for dissenters in the Metropolis)
OR B 1713-1854 (PRO: RG 4/3974-4001, 4288-91, 4633; RG 8/35-38; indexes RG 4/4652-57); B 1822-54, Internment Books B 1789-1854 (GL); B 1823-54 (SG)
Cop Index to B 1788-1853 (Mf, 1998)
see under **ISLINGTON** Upper Street *for* New Bunhill Fields

ST LUKE OLD STREET (46,642) [Ossulstone Hundred; Holborn Union from 1869] (created from St Giles Cripplegate, 1733) (Peculiar of the Dean and Chapter of St Paul's until 1845) (transferred to London, 1889)
OR C 1733-1966, M 1733-1965, B 1733-1854 (LMA)
BT 1813, 1816 (LMA)
Cop C 1742-65, M 1742-64 (SG); M 1783-1800 (I only SG); C 1742-65, 1808, 1813-41, M 1742-1837, B 1742-55 (LMA); M 1742-50 (Boyd); C 1742-66, 1799-1841, B 1762-63 (I SG)

ST LUKE OLD STREET Independent Chapel, Pavement, Moorfields (later Pavement Chapel, New North Road, Shoreditch (Independent) f 1663
OR ZC 1778-1828 (PRO: RG 4/4340)

ST LUKE OLD STREET The Pest House (French Church) *fl.* 1706
OR no registers known

ST LUKE OLD STREET Bunhill Row (Independent)
OR C 1793-99 (PRO: RG 4/4479)

ST LUKE OLD STREET The Tabernacle, City Road (Independent) f 1756
OR ZC 1768-1840 (PRO: RG 4/4262, 4523)

ST LUKE OLD STREET City Road Church, City Road (Wesleyan Methodist) f 1777
OR B 1779-1840 (PRO: RG 4/4263-65, 4333, 4388); C 1838-1946, B 1779-84
   (LMA: acc.2330); B 1779-1854 (Ch Sec)
Cop B 1779-1854, 1858 (Ts I SG)
Cop (Mf) B 1779-1858 (Ptd, North Middlesex FHS, 1990)

ST LUKE OLD STREET Baptist Meeting, Mitchell Street f 1783
OR C 1787-1837 (PRO: RG 4/4174)

ST MARGARET WESTMINSTER, Broad Sanctuary (25,344) [City of Westminster;
   St Margaret and St John Union 1765-1867, St George Hanover Square Union 1867-89]
   (transferred to London, 1889)
OR C 1539-1987, M 1539-1987, Banns 1844-1958, B 1539-1853 (WPL)
BT 1813-17, 1822, 1840-42 (no M 1840-42) (LMA)
Cop CMB 1539-1660 (Ptd, A.M. Burke, 1914); C 1660-75, M 1664-75, B 1660-62
   (Ptd, HS 64, 1935); C 1876-81, M 1676-82, B 1664-66 (Ptd, HS 88, 1958);
   C 1681-88, M 1681-99, B 1666-73 (Ptd, HS 89, 1977); M 1676-1780 (C of A);
   M 1539-1660, c1701-75 (Boyd)

ST MARGARET WESTMINSTER Chapels Royal, Whitehall
OR ZC 1647-1875, M 1647-1880, ML 1687-1754, 1807, D 1647-1709
   (PRO: RG 8/76-78, 110; PRO 30/19/1; LC 5/211)
Cop CM 1704-1867 (C of A)

ST MARGARET WESTMINSTER Holy Trinity, Prince Consort Road, Knightsbridge
   (chapelry of St Margaret)
OR C 1666-94, 1866-1903, M 1658-1752, 1866-1903, Banns 1890-93 (WPL)
Cop M 1658-81 (Ptd, J.H. Bloom, 1925); C 1674-94, M 1689-1752 (Ts I SG);
   M 1658-81 (Boyd)

ST MARGARET WESTMINSTER Scotch Presbyterian Church, Peter Street (later
   Lisle Street, Leicester Square)
OR ZC 1741-1814 (PRO: RG 4/4160-61)

ST MARTIN IN THE FIELDS Burying Ground, Camden Town
OR in original registers of St Martin's
BT B 1813-55 (LMA)
Cop B 1806-56 (Ptd Mf, J. Alexander, 1985)

ST MARTIN IN THE FIELDS, Trafalgar Square, Westminster (23,732)
   [City of Westminster; Strand Union from 1868] (transferred to London, 1889)
OR C 1551-1965, M 1551-1968, Banns 1699-1725, 1729-1966, B 1551-1856 (WPL)
BT 1800-05, Mar 1808-09, Mar 1810-11, 1813-34, 1848-55 (no M 1848-55) (LMA)
Cop B 1525-1603 (from churchwardens' receipts) (Ptd, J.V. Kitto, 1901);
   CMB 1550-1619 (Ptd, HS 25, 1898); CMB 1619-36 (Ptd, HS 66, 1936); M 1636-95
   (GL: Challen 1, 42); M 1550-1619 (Boyd)

ST MARTIN IN THE FIELDS Meeting House, Peel's Court, John Street
(Society of Friends) (registers listed more fully in introduction)
OR Z 1644-1837, M 1663-1773, 1777-1836, B 1713-1837 (PRO: RG 6/417-18, 536, 591,
660, 695, 1079, 1098, 1106, 1137, 1436, 1489, 1563)
Cop Z 1644-1837, M 1663-1773, 1777-1836, B 1713-1837 (Friends' House)

ST MARTIN IN THE FIELDS Savoy (closed 1731), **Spring Gardens** (b 1685, closed
1755) and **Les Grecs** f c1681 in Newport Market, moved to Edward Street, 1822, and
to Shaftesbury Avenue (then Bloomsbury Street) 1845 and renamed **St Jean de Savoie**)
(French Churches)
OR C 1680, 1690, 1702-1900, M 1684-1753 (PRO: RG 4/4611, 4641-42, 4644)
Cop C 1680, 1690, 1702-1900, M 1684-1753 (Ptd, Hug Soc 26, 1922); C 1680, 1690,
1702-1900 (IGI); M 1684-1753 (Boyd)

ST MARTIN IN THE FIELDS Hungerford Market French Church (moved to Castle
Street, near Leicester Square, 1703)
OR C 1688-1754, M 1688-1754 (PRO: RG 4/4550)
Cop C 1688-1754, M 1688-1754 (Ptd, Hug Soc 21, 1928); C 1688-1754 (IGI);
M 1688-1754 (Boyd)

ST MARTIN IN THE FIELDS Independent Chapel, Orange Street, Leicester Square
f 1693
OR no registers known

ST MARTIN IN THE FIELDS German Lutheran Church, Savoy, Strand
OR ZC 1694-1771, 1777-1840, M 1694-1754, DB 1696-1840 (PRO: RG 4/4625-32)

ST MARTIN IN THE FIELDS Scotch Church, Crown Court, Russell Street f 1700
OR C 1711-97, 1837-1958, M 1917-52 (Scottish Record Office: CH 2/852/1,15-24);
ZC 1794-1837 (PRO: RG 4/4232)

ST MARTIN IN THE FIELDS Adelphi, James Street (Lady Huntingdon's) f 1790
OR C 1790-91, 1797-1837 (PRO: RG 4/4215)

ST MARYLEBONE Middlesex Hospital f 1745 in Windmill Street, St Pancras, moved
1755 to Mortimer Street, St Marylebone
OR ZC 1747-57, 1894-1930 (LMA); ZC 1757-1807 (Hospital)
Cop ZC 1747-1807 (Ts I LMA, SG)

ST MARYLEBONE Workhouse Chapel, Northumberland Street
OR C 1790-1810, 1839-65 (LMA)
Cop C 1839-65 (IGI)
Cop (Mf) C 1839-65 (SLC, LMA)

ST MARYLEBONE St Marylebone, Marylebon Road (originally called Tyburn)
(122,206) [Ossulstone Hundred; St Marylebone Union] (transferred to London, 1889)
OR C 1679-1925, M !668-1923, B 1668-1888 (LMA)
BT 1629 (GL); 1813-33 (LMA)
Cop M 1668-1754 (Ptd, HS 47, 1917); M 1754-75 (Ptd, HS 48, 1918); M 1775-83
(Ptd, HS 51, 1921); M 1783-92 (Ptd, HS 52, 1922); M 1792-96 (Ptd, HS 53, 1923);
M 1796-1801 (Ptd, HS 54, 1924); M 1801-06 (Ptd, HS 55, 1925); M 1806-09
(Ptd, HS 56, 1926); M 1809-12 (Ptd, HS 57, 1927); M 1629 (Ts I GL, LMA, SG,
CRW); C 1811, 1828-33, M 1796-1837 (Ts I only, SG); M 1668-1812 (Boyd)

ST MARYLEBONE **Oxford Chapel**, Vere Street, Mayfair
OR M 1736-54 (LMA)
Cop M 1736-54 (Ptd, HS 47, 1917); M 1736-54 (Boyd)

ST MARYLEBONE **All Souls**, Langham Place (created from St Marylebone, 1825)
(transferred to London, 1889)
OR C 1825-1916, M 1825-1918 (LMA)
BT CM 1825-36 (LMA)

ST MARYLEBONE **Christ Church**, Cosway Place (created from St Marylebone, 1825)
(transferred to London, 1889)
OR C 1825-1939, M 1825-1957, B 1825-53 (LMA)
BT 1825-34 (no B 1825, 1829) (LMA)
Cop M 1825-28 (Ts SG); C 1825-37, M 1825-37 (Ts I only, SG); B 1825-53 (Ts I SG)

ST MARYLEBONE **St Mary, Bryanstone Square** (created from St Marylebone, 1825)
(transferred to London, 1889)
OR C 1825-1928, M 1825-1963 (LMA)
BT CM 1825-37 (LMA)
Cop C 1825-1963, M 1825-1962 (Ts I only, SG)

ST MARYLEBONE **Holy Trinity**, Marylebone Road and Albany Street (created from
St Marylebone, 1825) (transferred to London, 1889)
OR C 1828-1904, M 1828-1942, B 1829-53 (LMA)
BT 1828-39 (no M 1838-39, no B 1828) (LMA)
Cop B 1829-53 (Ts I SG)

ST MARYLEBONE **Marylebone Chapel** (French Church) *fl.* 1656
OR no registers known

ST MARYLEBONE **Russian Orthodox Church**, Welbeck Street, Cavendish Square
OR C 1721-46, 1750-63, 1782-1927, M 1721-46, 1749-55, 1782-1927, B 1753-63,
1782-1927 (PRO: RG 8/111-304)

ST MARYLEBONE **Scotch Church**, Wells Street, Oxford Street f 1750
OR ZC 1753-1837 (PRO: RG 4/4205); C 1753-1875 (Presbyterian Historical Society)

ST MARYLEBONE **Blandford Street Independent Chapel**, Portman Square
OR C 1782-1820 (LMA: R.969)
Cop Z 1782-1820 (Ts GL, SG, WPL)

ST MARYLEBONE **Providence Chapel**, Tichfield Street (later in Grays Inn Lane)
(Independent)
OR ZC 1784-1835 (PRO: RG 4/4240-42)

ST MARYLEBONE **St James**, Spanish Place, Manchester Square. This was originally the
Spanish Embassy Chapel. It had been in various places from its foundation in the 17th
century. (Roman Catholic) b 1791 (Cath Dir 1965)
OR CM 1732+, D 1857-63, 1876-78 (Inc)
Cop C 1732-1848, M 1732-1845 (SG); M 1732-1845 (I Institute of Heraldic &
Genealogical Studies, Canterbury)

ST MARYLEBONE **Wesleyan Chapel**, Hinde Street, Manchester Square f 1812
OR ZC 1813-37 (PRO: RG 4/4339); C 1836-37, M 1864-1964 (WPL)

ST MARYLEBONE St Mary, Sandwich Street (Lutheran)
OR Roll of communicants 1811-17 (WPL)

ST MARYLEBONE Independent Calvinist Chapel, Titchfield Street (formerly
   Eschol Chapel, Marshall Street, St James Westminster)
OR C 1815-47 (PRO: RG 4/4355)

ST MARYLEBONE French Chapel, Little George Street, King Street, Portman Square
   (Roman Catholic) (Cath Dir 1828)

ST MARYLEBONE York Street (Presbyterian) f 1824 to Little Portland Street, 1833
OR C 1825-37 (PRO: RG 4/4409)

ST MARYLEBONE Mount Zion Chapel, St John's Wood Road (Baptist) f 1826
OR no registers known

ST MARYLEBONE Salisbury Street Wesleyan Methodist Chapel
OR ZC 1828-37 (PRO: RG 4/4213); C 1838-81 (WPL)
Cop C 1828-37 (Ts GL, SG, WPL)

ST MARYLEBONE Irvingite Church, Newman Street, Oxford Street
OR ZC 1832-40 (PRO: RG 4/4249, 4533)

ST MARYLEBONE Our Lady, Lisson Grove, St John's Wood (Roman Catholic) f 1833
   (Cath Dir 1965)
OR CM 1836+, B 1858-61, 1911 (Inc)
Cop M 1856-70 (I Institute of Heraldic & Genealogical Studies, Canterbury)

ST MARY LE STRAND, near Somerset House, Westminster [City of Westminster;
   Strand Union] (transferred to London, 1889)
OR C 1558-1882, M 1558-1990, Banns 1653-69, 1771-1808, B 1558-1853 (WPL)
BT 1800-50, 1852-59 (no M 1838-59, B 1854-59) (LMA)
Cop M 1606-25 (Ptd, *Genealogist* NS 4-5, 1887-88); M 1653-56 (Ptd, *Genealogist*
   NS 10, 1894); M 1603-25 (Ptd, *New York Genealogical and Biographical Record* 18,
   1887 - no copy at SG); M 1558-1754 (GL: Challen 15, SG); M 1606-1754 (Boyd)

ST MARY LE STRAND Somerset House Chapel (Roman Catholic) (previously at
   St James Palace, and later Portuguese Embassy Chapel)
OR C 1671-95, M 1671-95 (Portuguese Embassy)
Cop M 1662-1849 (Ptd, CRS 38, 1941)

ST MARY LE STRAND Somerset House Chapel (Protestant)
OR C 1732-75, M 1714-76, B 1720-70 (PRO: RG 8/109)
Cop C 1732-75, M 1714-76, B 1720-70 (Ptd, T. Phillips, 1831 and James Coleman,
   1862); M 1714-76 (Boyd); C 1732-75, M 1714-76 (IGI)

ST MARY LE STRAND Denmark Court (Western) Synagogue, Strand f 1761
   Great Pulteney Street, 1765-1826 at Denmark Court, 1826 to St Alban's Place,
   Haymarket, demolished 1914, to Alfred Place, Tottenham Court Road, destroyed 1941
OR no registers known, probably destroyed by enemy action, 1941
Cop ZMD 1811-72 (Jewish Museum); 1761-1932 (catalogue only, ptd, C. Roth, 1932)

ST PANCRAS Foundling Hospital, Guilford Street
OR C 1741-57, 1760-1838, M 1754, B 1741-59 (PRO: RG 4/4238, 4396);
   C 1741-1885, B 1741-58 (LMA: A/FH)

ST PANCRAS Middlesex Hospital, Windmill Street f 1745 moved to Mortimer Street, St Marylebone 1755 (q.v.)

ST PANCRAS Workhouse, Kings Road
OR Z 1834-41, 1843-51, 1871-1914, D 1853-63 (in registers) (LMA)
Cop C 1834-75 (IGI)
Cop (Mf) C 1834-75 (SLC, LMA)

ST PANCRAS St Pancras, Euston Road (103,548) [Ossulstone Hundred; St Pancras Union] (transferred to London, 1889)
OR C 1660-1936, M 1660-1950, B 1689-1854 (LMA)
BT 1813-80 (no M 1838-80, no B 1856-80) (LMA)
Cop C 1660-1752, B 1689-1752 (SG); M 1660-1754 (GL: Challen 22, SG);
    C 1830, M 1836-37, B 1796-1807 (I only SG); C 1752-93, M 1660-1754, B 1752-93
    (LMA); C 1802-37, M 1754-1816, 1824-42, B 1793-1810 (Ts I only, SG); M 1701-54
    (Boyd); C1802-16, 1826-37, M 1753, B 1753-73 (I, SG)

ST PANCRAS Percy Chapel, Charlotte Street
OR C 1747-53, 1766-1808 (very few 1794-1808) (LMA)

ST PANCRAS Fitzroy Chapel, London Street, later St Saviour, Maple Street,
    Fitzroy Square (created from St John the Evangelist, Charlotte Street, St Pancras, 1865,
    reunited to it, 1904)
OR C 1779-96, 1804-05, 1865-1913, M 1865-1913 (LMA)

ST PANCRAS St John the Baptist, Highgate Road, Kentish Town,
    formerly **Kentish Town Chapel** (created from St Pancras, 1863)
OR C 1804-1961, M 1754-89, B 1822-54 (LMA)

ST PANCRAS All Saints, Camden Street, Camden Town, formerly **Camden Chapel**
    (created from St Pancras, 1852)
OR C 1824-47, M 1858-1947 (LMA)

ST PANCRAS St Mary the Virgin, Eversholt Street, Somers Town,
    formerly **Somers Town Chapel** (created from St Pancras, 1852)
OR C 1826-29 (LMA); C 1829+, M 1869+ (Inc)

ST PANCRAS St Peter, Regent Square, formerly **Regent Square Chapel** (created from
    St Pancras, 1852)
OR C 1829-1943, M 1858-1941 (LMA)

ST PANCRAS Christ Church, Albany Street (created from St Pancras, 1837) (transferred
    to London, 1889)
OR C 1837-1969, M 1846-1960 (LMA)
BT C 1837-49 (LMA)

ST PANCRAS Baptist Chapel, Ampton Street or Cubitt Street, Kings Cross f 1646
OR no registers known

ST PANCRAS Tottenham Court Chapel, Tottenham Court Road (now **Whitfield
    Memorial Church**) (Independent) f 1756
OR ZC 1805-40 (PRO: RG 4/4200); C 1880-99, M 1883-98, B 1790-1838
    (LMA: acc.1801/1-4)

ST PANCRAS French Chapel, Conway Street, Fitzroy Square f 1796 closed 1814
OR CM 1798-1814 (Archives de Nantes)

ST PANCRAS St Aloysius, Phoenix Road, Somers Town (Roman Catholic) f 1798
(Cath Dir 1965)
OR C 1808+, M 1837+ (Inc); B 1857-59 (Westminster Diocesan Archives)
Cop M 1837-70 (I Institute of Heraldic & Genealogical Studies, Canterbury);
B 1857-59 (Catholic FHS); C 1808-39 (Ts SG)

ST PANCRAS Kentish Town Chapel, Kelley Street (Independent) f 1807
OR records with Church Secretary

ST PANCRAS Camden Town (Independent) f 1815
OR ZC 1817-37 (PRO: RG 4/4384)

ST PANCRAS Wesleyan Chapel, Gloucester Place, Kentish Town f 1816
OR ZC 1817-36 (PRO: RG 4/4532)

ST PANCRAS Baptist Chapel, Henrietta Street, Brunswick Square f 1817
OR B 1828-37 (PRO: RG 4/4338)

ST PANCRAS Caledonian Chapel, Regent Square (formerly Cross Street, Hatton Garden)
(Scotch Church) f 1822
OR ZC 1822-55 (PRO: RG 4/4285, 4312)

ST PANCRAS Wesleyan Chapel, Liverpool Street, Kings Cross f 1823
OR ZC 1820-40, B 1837 (PRO: RG 4/4192, 4276, 4343)

ST PANCRAS Bethel Chapel, Somers Town (Baptist) f 1826
OR no registers known

ST PANCRAS Albany Chapel, Frederick Street, Regents Park (Independent) f 1835
OR ZC 1835-37 (PRO: RG 4/4397)

ST PETER ad VINCULA (Chapel Royal in Tower of London)
OR CM 1538+, B 1538-1871 (Chaplain)
BT none
Cop Extr (C of A: Chester Mss 8, pp.191-235)

ST SEPULCHRE Holborn (4,769) (part City of London, part Ossulstone Hundred,
Middlesex; West London Union 1837-45, Holborn Union from 1845]
OR C 1662-1886, M 1662-1901, B 1662-1857 (GL)
BT 1800-41, 1843-60, 1862-86, 1888, 1890 (no M 1862-90, B 1858-90) (LMA)
Cop B 1813-53 (CLBI 2)

SAVOY Precinct of the (Queen's Chapel of the Savoy) St John the Baptist later St Mary
(431) [City of Westminster; Strand Union] (transferred to London, 1889)
OR CMB 1680+ (Inc)
Cop [? Extr] CMB 1680-1827 (C of A)

SERJEANTS' INN, Chancery Lane (31 in 1821; none given in 1831; 5 in 1841)
(extra-parochial) (Inn of Court) sold 1877 and merged in Fleet Street Serjeants' Inn

SERJEANTS' INN, Fleet Street (104) (extra-parochial) (Inn of Court)

SHADWELL St Paul, The Highway (9,544) [Ossulstone Hundred; Stepney Union]
(transferred to London, 1889) (created from Stepney, 1670)
OR C 1670-1927, M 1671-1934, B 1670-1903 (LMA)
BT C 1663, B 1663-64 (GL); 1800, 1807-12, 1823, 1827-53 (no M 1845-53) (LMA)
Cop M 1671-1754 (GL: Challen 13); M 1671-1800 (SG); C 1813-37, M 1671-1812,
1836-37 (Ts I only, SG); M 1671-1754 (Boyd)

SHEPPERTON St Nicholas, Church Square (847) [Spelthorne Hundred; Staines Union]
(transferred to Surrey 1965)
OR CMB 1574+ (Inc)
BT 1629-30 (GL); 1829-54 (no M 1838-54) (LMA)
Cop C 1574-1846, M 1574-1850, B 1574-1866 (Ts CRW, SG); M 1629-30 (Ts I GL,
LMA, SG, CRW)

SHOREDITCH Hoxton Cemetery, Hoxton Street (Jewish)
OR B 1707-1878 (United Synagogue Burial Society, Upper Woburn Place, WC1)
Cop B 1707-1878 (part transcript at Burial Society)

SHOREDITCH Aske's Hospital Chapel, Hoxton
OR C 1731-67, 1839, M 1696-1754, B 1724-1852, 1854 (GL)
Cop C 1731-1839, M 1696-1754, B 1724-1852 (SG); C 1731-44 (IGI)

SHOREDITCH Geffery's Almshouses Chapel, Kingsland Road
OR B 1794-1850 (GL)

SHOREDITCH Workhouse, Kingsland Road
OR C 1820-71, B 1820-28 (GL); Z 1862-72, 1887-91, D 1872-85 (LMA)
Cop Z 1836-75 (IGI)
Cop (Mf) Z 1836-75 (SLC)

SHOREDITCH St Leonard, High Street (68,564) [Ossulstone Hundred; Shoreditch Union]
(transferred to London, 1889)
OR C 1558-1928, M 1558-1930, Banns 1754-56, B 1558-1858 (GL)
BT 1807-18, 1827-35 (LMA); 1630, 1639, 1665, 1818-19, 1828-29, 1831-32
(no MB 1832) (GL)
Cop (Mf) C 1558-1745, 1871-1901, M 1558-1764, 1808-12, 1875-99, B 1558-1858,
Workhouse C 1820-71, B 1778-1828 (SG)
Cop C 1694-1709 (Ts CRW, SG); M 1754-91, 1827-37 (Ms I only GL)

SHOREDITCH St John the Baptist, New North Road, Hoxton (created from Shoreditch
St Leonard, 1830) (transferred to London, 1889)
OR CM 1830-1920, B 1826-68 (LMA)
Cop C 1830-41, M 1830-37, 1851-52, B 1826-40 (Ts I only, SG)

SHOREDITCH St Mary, Haggerston Road, Haggerston (created from Shoreditch
St Leonard, 1830) (transferred to London, 1889)
OR C 1830-1921, 1942-49, M 1830-1940, 1944-49, B 1829-64 (LMA)
Cop C 1830-37, M 1830-37 (Ts I only, SG)

SHOREDITCH St Mary, Moorfields (Roman Catholic)
OR C 1763+, M 1750+ (Westminster Cathedral Archives)
Cop C 1763-1817, 1823-27, 1832-39, M 1750-53, 1763-1821, 1837-56 (Ts SG,
Catholic FHS)

SHOREDITCH Pavement Chapel, New North Road (formerly in the Pavement, Moorfields) (Independent) f 1663
OR ZC 1778-1828 (PRO: RG 4/4340)

SHOREDITCH French Church, Swan Fields
OR C 1721-35, M 1722-31 (PRO: RG 4/4648)
Cop C 1721-35, M 1722-31 (Ptd, Hug Soc 45, 1956); M 1722-31 (Boyd); C 1721-35 (IGI)

SHOREDITCH Hoxton Chapel (French Church)
OR C 1751-83, M 1748-53 (PRO: RG 4/4559)
Cop C 1751-83, M 1748-53 (Ptd, Hug Soc 45, 1956); M 1748-53 (Boyd); C 1751-83 (IGI)

SHOREDITCH Baptist Chapel, Worship Street f 1779
OR B 1785-1837 (PRO: RG 4/4515)

SHOREDITCH Holywell Mount Chapel, Chapel Street, Curtain Road (Independent) f 1777
OR ZC 1783-1837 (PRO: RG 4/4257, 4412, 4508); CB 1837-54 (LMA)

SHOREDITCH Calvinist Methodist Chapel, Cumberland Street, Curtain Road
OR ZC 1788-1815 (PRO: RG 4/4509)

SHOREDITCH Independent Chapel, Kingsland f 1794
OR C 1795-1848, B 1826-43 (PRO: RG 4/4344)

SHOREDITCH Academy Chapel, Hoxton Street
OR ZC 1800-36 (PRO: RG 4/4530)

SHOREDITCH Wesleyan Chapel, Hoxton Old Town f 1800
OR ZC 1817-37 (PRO: RG 4/4246)

SHOREDITCH Gloucester Chapel, New Haggerstone (Independent) f 1818
OR ZC 1814-37 (PRO: RG 4/4315, 4413, 4510)

SHOREDITCH Baptist Chapel, Homerton Row, Homerton f 1820
OR no registers known

SHOREDITCH Ebenezer Chapel, Old Street Road (Bible Christian) f 1823
OR ZC 1823-37 (PRO: RG 4/4162)

SHOREDITCH The Tabernacle, Hackney Road (Baptist) f 1835
OR no registers known

SHOREDITCH Gloucester Chapel, Haggerston
OR C 1837-59, B 1837-52 (PRO: RG 8/69)

SOHO St Anne, Dean Street (15,600) [City of Westminster; Strand Union 1836-68, Westminster Union from 1868] (transferred to London, 1889) (created from St Martin in the Fields, 1687)
OR C 1686-1931, M 1686-1940, Banns 1754-75, 1784-1839, 1846-59, 1869-1902, B 1686-1853 (WPL)
BT 1800-10, 1813-33, 1835-53 (no M 1852-53, B 1851-53) (LMA)
Cop C 1789-1808, B 1788-1808 (SG); M 1686-1754 (GL: Challen 15; Bpsgate Lib); C 1686-1721, M 1686-1709, B 1686-92 (Ms WPL); M 1686-1754 (Boyd)

SOHO La Patente de Soho alias Le Temple f 1689 in Berwick Street moved to
    Little Chapel Street 1694, united to Le Grecs 1784 (French Church)
OR C 1689-1782, M 1689-1753 (PRO: RG 4/4639)
Cop C 1689-1782, M 1689-1753 (Ptd, Hug Soc 45, 1956); C 1689-1782 (IGI);
    M 1689-1753 (Boyd)

SOHO La Carré French Church, Berwick Street
OR C 1690-1788, M 1690-1753 (PRO: RG 4/4545-46, 4548)
Cop C 1690-1788, M 1690-1753 (Ptd, Hug Soc 25, 1921); C 1690-1788 (IGI);
    M 1690-1753 (Boyd)

SOHO The Tabernacle, Milk Alley f c1693 closed c1720, united to Leicester Fields,
    St James Piccadilly
OR C 1696-1719, M 1696-1719 (PRO: RG 4/4547)
Cop C 1696-1719, M 1696-1719 (Ptd, Hug Soc 29, 1926); C 1696-1719 (IGI);
    M 1696-1719 (Boyd)

SOHO Rider's Court French Church opened 1700, closed c1738
OR C 1700-47, M 1700-38 (PRO: RG 4/4607-08)
Cop C 1700-47, M 1700-38 (Ptd, Hug Soc 30, 1927); C 1700-47 (IGI); M 1700-38 (Boyd)

SOHO Le Petit Charenton, Grafton Street (French Church)
OR C 1701-05, M 1701-05 (PRO: RG 4/4610)
Cop C 1701-05, M 1701-05 (Ptd, Hug Soc 32, 1929)

SOHO Scotch Presbyterian Church, Lisle Street, Leicester Square (formerly
    at Peter Street, Westminster)
OR ZC 1741-1814 (PRO: RG 4/4160-61)

SOHO Venetian Embassy Chapel, Soho Square (Roman Catholic)
OR C 1744-96, M 1744-54. 1772-88 (Westminster Diocesan Archives)
Cop C 1744-96, M 1744-54, 1772-88 (Ts I SG)

SOHO Swiss Church, Moor Street, Soho Square
OR C 1762-1839 (PRO: RG 4/4638)

SOHO Independent Chapel, Crown Street
OR ZC 1785-1837 (PRO: RG 4/4301)

SOHO St Patrick, Sutton Street, Soho Square (Roman Catholic) f 1792 (Cath Dir 1965)
OR C 1790-1899, M 1809-1937, B 1858-1902 (Westminster Diocesan Archives);
    C 1899+, M 1937+ (Inc)
Cop C 1790-1851, M 1809-56 (Catholic FHS, SG); M 1861-70 (I Institute of Heraldic &
    Genealogical Studies, Canterbury)

SOHO Independent Chapel, Little Chapel Street f 1796
OR ZC 1796-1836 (PRO: RG 4/4346)

SOHO Wardour Street Chapel, Wardour Street (Methodist)
OR C 1796-1894 (LMA: N/M/11)

SOHO Wesleyan Chapel, Peter Street f 1817
OR ZC 1826-38 (PRO: RG 4/4252)

SPA FIELDS *see* **CLERKENWELL Spa Fields**

SPITALFIELDS Christ Church, Commercial Street (17,949) [Ossulstone Hundred; Whitechapel Union] (transferred to London, 1889) (created from Stepney, 1729)
OR C 1729-1898, M 1729-1902, B 1729-1859 (LMA)
BT 1800-53 (no M 1838-53) (LMA)
Cop C 1767-95, M 1805-28 (Ts I only SG); C 1763-1837, M 1729-1837 (Ts I only, SG)
Cop (Mf) Banns 1833-61 (Index, Mf, ELFHS, 1991)

SPITALFIELDS St Jean, John Street (French Church) f 1687 closed 1827
OR C 1687-1823, M 1687-1751 (PRO: RG 4/4578-80, 4590-92, 4635-36)
Cop C 1687-1823, M 1687-1751 (Ptd, Hug Soc 39, 1938); C 1687-1823 (IGI); M 1687-1751 (Boyd)

SPITALFIELDS Répertoire Générale (Huguenot community general register)
OR C 1689-1774 (La Patente); C 1695-1715 (Crispin Street); C 1703-42 (Wheeler Street); C 1719 (Le Marché); C 1709-16 (Bell Lane); C 1719-40 (Brown's Lane) (PRO: RG 4/4637)
Cop C 1689-1774 (Ptd, Hug Soc 45, 1956); C 1689-1774 (IGI)

SPITALFIELDS La Patente de Spitalfields or La Nouvelle Patente, Paternoster Row, later Brown's Lane f 1689 (French Church)
OR C 1689-1785, M 1689-1753 (PRO: RG 4/4596, 4602, 4614-16)
Cop C 1689-1785, M 1689-1753 (Ptd, Hug Soc 11, 1898); C 1689-1785 (IGI); M 1689-1753 (Boyd)

SPITALFIELDS Petticoat Lane French Church *fl.* 1691 joined the Artillery 1695
OR no registers known

SPITALFIELDS Church of the Artillery, Artillery Lane reb 1763, closed 1786 (later a synagogue) and united to Threadneedle Street (French Church)
OR C 1691-1786, M 1691-1754, Banns 1713-33 (PRO: RG 4/4560, 4576, 4593-94, 4612)
Cop C 1691-1786, M 1691-1754 (Ptd, Hug Soc 42, 1948); M 1691-1754 (Boyd); C 1691-1786 (IGI)

SPITALFIELDS French Church, Crispin Street f 1694 closed 1717 united to La Patente de Spitalfields
OR C 1694-1716, M 1694-1716 (PRO: RG 4/4562-63)
Cop C 1694-1716, M 1694-1716 (Ptd, Hug Soc 32, 1929); C 1694-1716 (IGI); M 1694-1716 (Boyd)

SPITALFIELDS French Church, Pearl Street f 1697 closed 1701
OR C 1698-1701, M 1698-1701 (PRO: RG 4/4562)
Cop C 1698-1701, M 1698-1701 (Ptd, Hug Soc 32, 1929); C 1698-1701 (IGI); M 1698-1701 (Boyd)

SPITALFIELDS French Church, Wheeler Street f 1703 closed 1742 and united to La Patente de Spitalfields
OR C 1703-41, M 1704-41 (PRO: RG 4/4561, 4595, 4606, 4613)
Cop C 1703-41, M 1704-41 (Ptd, Hug Soc 45, 1956); C 1703-41 (IGI); M 1704-41 (Boyd)

SPITALFIELDS Eglise Neuve, Church Street (French Church)
OR C 1753-1809 (PRO: RG 4/4589)

SPITALFIELDS White's Row Church (formerly Bishopsgate Street Chapel)
OR C 1756-1837 (PRO: RG 4/4210, 4537); C 1756-1908 (LMA)

SPITALFIELDS Baptist Chapel, Church Street f 1785
OR Z 1772-1826 (PRO: RG 4/4522)

SPITALFIELDS Independent Chapel, Hope Street f 1787
OR ZC 1830-36 (PRO: RG 4/4471)

SPITALFIELDS Wesleyan Chapel, Church Street
OR ZC 1815-37 (PRO: RG 4/4323); C 1838-90 (LMA)

STAINES St Peter later St Mary the Virgin (2,486) [Spelthorne Hundred; Staines Union]
    (transferred to Surrey 1965)
OR C 1539-1665, 1692-1958, M 1539-1750, 1755-1962, Banns 1754-81, 1785-87,
    1894-1905, 1912-62, B 1538-1682, 1772-1948 (LMA: DRO 2); CB 1653-91,
    M 1653-60 (BL: Egerton Ms 2004)
BT 1800-Mar 1809, Mar 1810-Apr 1868, Feb 1870-Apr 1871, Feb 1872-73
    (no M 1863-73) (LMA)
Cop C 1644-94, MB 1653-60 (Ptd Crisp, 1887); M 1653-60 (Boyd); C 1644-94 (IGI);
    M 1813-37 (WMI)

STAINES Meeting House, Quaker's Lane, Blackboy Lane or Goodman Place (Quaker)
    b 1712, reb 1844, 1937

STAINES Independent Chapel, Kingston Road f 1789 b 1802 in Tilley's Lane, reb in
    Thames Street, 1837
OR ZC 1785-1837 (PRO: RG 4/1948, 2461)
Cop ZC 1785-1837 (Ptd Mf, CRW and NMFHS, 1985)
Cop (Mf) ZC 1785-1837 (SLC)

STAINES Baptist Chapel, Bridge Street f by c1778 in Church Street, reb in Bridge
    Street, 1837
OR no registers known

STANMORE, GREAT St John the Evangelist, Church End (1,144) [Gore Hundred;
    Hendon Union]
OR C 1599-1885, M 1599-1906, Banns 1823-80, 1902-39, B 1599-1934 (LMA: DRO 14)
BT 1800-Mar 1811, Mar 1812-67 (no M 1852-67) (LMA)
Cop M 1599-1837 (Ptd, Phillimore 6, 1914); C 1599-1834, B 1599-1928 (LMA)

STANMORE, LITTLE St Lawrence alias Whitchurch, Whitchurch Lane (867)
    [Gore Hundred; Hendon Union]
OR C 1558-1962, M 1558-1956, Banns 1754-1812, 1843-89, 1900-71, B 1558-1963
    (LMA: DRO 107)
BT 1630, 1639 (GL); 1800-09, 1811-68 (no M 1853, 1855-68) (LMA)
Cop CMB 1558-1840 (Harrow Loc. Stud. Lib); M 1630, 1639 (Ts GL, LMA, SG, CRW)

STANMORE, LITTLE Edgware Chapel (Independent) f 1834
OR ZC 1834-37, B 1835 (PRO: RG 4/1324)
Cop ZC 1834-37, B 1835 (Ptd Mf, CRW and NMFHS, 1985)
Cop (Mf) ZC 1834-37, B 1835 (SLC)

STANWELL St Mary the Virgin, High Street (1,386) [Spelthorne Hundred; Staines Union] (transferred to Surrey 1965)
OR C 1632-1916 (Colebrook Chapel C 1623-37), M 1633-1919, Banns 1760-1872, 1964-67, B 1637-1917 (LMA: DRO 42)
BT 1630 (GL); 1800-Apr 1812, Dec 1812-33, 1835-38, 1840-69 (no M 1838-69) (LMA)
Cop M 1632-1812 (Ptd, Phillimore 4, 1912); M 1630, 1813-37 (Ts I GL, LMA, SG, CRW); C 1787-1812 (I only SG); M 1813-37 (WMI); M 1632-1812 (Boyd); M 1790-1812 (Pallot Index)
Cop (Mf) C 1632-1916, M 1633-1919, B 1637-1917 (LMA)

STANWELL Poyle Chapel (Independent) f 1807, b 1823
OR ZC 1820-37, B 1826-35 (PRO: RG 4/1132, 2568)
Cop ZC 1820-37, B 1826-35 (Ptd, Mf WSFHS MS 5)
Cop (Mf) ZC 1820-37, B 1826-35 (SLC)

STANWELL Independent Chapel b 1810 closed 1860s
OR no registers known

STAPLE INN (58) (extra-parochial place) (Inn of Court) [Ossulstone Hundred; Holborn Union] sold 1884

STEPNEY Sephardi Velho (Old) Cemetery, Mile End Road (Jewish)
OR B 1657-1742 (Spanish & Portuguese Burial Society, Ashworth Road, W9)
Cop B 1657-1742 (Ptd, *Misc. Transactions of The Jewish Historical Society of England* 6, 1962)

STEPNEY Alderney Road Cemetery, Alderney Road (Jewish)
OR B 1697-1852 (United Synagogue Burial Society, Upper Woburn Place. London W9 1JY)

STEPNEY Sephardi Neuvo (New) Cemetery, Mile End Road (Jewish)
OR B 1733+ (Spanish & Portuguese Burial Society, Ashworth Road)
Cop B 1733-1918 (Ptd, ed. M.Rodrigues-Pereira, Bevis Marks Records 6, 1998)

STEPNEY Jewish Burial Ground, Brady Street
OR B 1796-1858 (Office of Chief Rabbi)

STEPNEY Bancroft Road Cemetery, Bancroft Road (Jewish)
OR B c1810-1920 (registers destroyed by enemy action, 1941)

STEPNEY St Dunstan, Stepney High Street (51,023) [Ossulstone Hundred; Stepney Union] (consists of the three hamlets of Mile End Old Town, Mile End New Town and Ratcliff) (transferred to London, 1889)
OR C 1568-1954, M 1568-1962, B 1568-1929 (LMA)
BT 1800-25, 1829-31 (LMA)
Cop M 1568-1719 (Ptd, T. Colyer-Fergusson, 3 vols., 1898-1901); C 1745-72, M 1791-1824 (Ts I only SG); C 1746-1837, M 1568-1837 (Ts I only, SG); M 1568-1754 (Boyd); B 1839-45 (I SG)
Cop (Mf) M 1719-54 (Kent FHS, Record Publications 143, 1985); C 1568-1770, 1798-1875, M 1719-1875, B 1622-1875 (SG)

STEFNEY Baptist Chapel, James Street (previously meeting in Wapping, then in James Street, then in Little Prescot Street, Goodmans Fields) f 1633
OR Z 1786-1803 (PRO: RG 4/4283)

STEPNEY Independent Meeting House, Bull Lane f 1644
OR ZC 1644-1837, M 1646-77, B 1780-1837 (PRO: RG 4/4414)
Cop M 1646-77 (Ts CRW, SG)

STEPNEY Latimer Chapel, Bridge Street formerly **Mile End Road Chapel** f 1671
OR ZC 1825-37 (PRO: RG 4/4526); other records destroyed in World War II

STEPNEY Meeting House, Ratcliff (Society of Friends) (registers listed more fully in introduction)
OR Z 1656-1806, M 1657-1820, B 1666-1821 (PRO: RG 6/419-20, 512, 537, 669, 674-76, 686, 1400, 1533-34)
Cop Z 1656-1806, M 1657-1820, B 1666-1821 (Friends' House)

STEPNEY Queen Street Meeting (Independent) f 1698
OR ZC 1698-1837, B 1822 (PRO: RG 4/4284, 4311)

STEPNEY Scotch Church, St Vincent Street, Mile End Old Town (until 1823 Broad Street, St George in the East)
OR ZC 1741-1840 (PRO: RG 4/4324-25)

STEPNEY Rose Lane Chapel (united with Queen Street Chapel, 1834), Ratcliff (Independent) f 1785
OR ZC 1785-1834, B 1786-1833 (PRO: RG 4/4259)

STEPNEY Coverly Fields Chapel, Mile End New Town f 1782
OR B 1815-54 (PRO: RG 4/4197-98, 4248, 4503-04); C 1782-1831, B 1802, 1816 (PRO: RG 8/71)

STEPNEY St Mary and St Michael, Commercial Road (Roman Catholic)
OR C 1789-1800, 1832-56 (Westminster Diocesan Archives)
Cop C 1789-1800 (Catholic FHS, SG); C 1832-40 (SG)

STEPNEY Sion Church, Union Street, Mile End Old Town (Lady Huntingdon's Connexion) f 1790
OR ZC 1791-1837 (PRO: RG 4/4196, 4517-21)

STEPNEY Cannon Street Road Congregational Chapel
OR C 1792-1810 (LMA: N/C/22)

STEPNEY Chapel (Independent) f 1796
OR C 1796-1820 (PRO: RG 8/70)

STEPNEY St Boniface (German Church), Adler Street, Commercial Road (Great St Thomas Apostle Bow Lane until 1859) (Roman Catholic) f 1809 (Cath Dir 1965)
OR C 1809+, M 1864+, D 1876+ (Inc)
Cop C 1809-1950, M 1864-1968 (Anglo-German FHS)

STEPNEY New Road Meeting House (Independent)
OR C 1811-17, B 1785-1810 (LMA: N/C/23)

STEPNEY Globe Fields Burial Ground (Wesleyan Methodist) f 1820
OR B 1820-57 (PRO: RG 4/4258, 4286-87)

STEPNEY Brunswick Chapel, Three Colt Street (Methodist)
OR C 1909-63, B 1831-53 (LMA: N/M/42/30-68)

STOKE NEWINGTON Cemetery *see* **HACKNEY** **Abney Park Cemetery**

STOKE NEWINGTON **St Mary**, Stoke Newington Church Street (3,480) [Ossulstone
Hundred; Hackney Union] (transferred to London, 1889)
OR C 1559-1942, M 1560-1977, B 1559-1851 (LMA)
BT 1813-26, 1829-35 (LMA)
Cop CB 1559-1812, M 1560-1812 (Hackney Archives Dept); M 1560-1812 (SG);
M 1560-1775, 1801-12 (Boyd)

STOKE NEWINGTON Newington Green (Presbyterian) f 1686 b 1708
OR CMD 1841-89; church rolls 1708-1976 (Hackney Archives Dept)

STOKE NEWINGTON **Independent Chapel**, Church Street f 1662
OR ZC 1785-1836, B 1838-52 (PRO: RG 4/4172-73)

STRATFORD LE BOW **St Mary**, Bow Road (3,371) [Ossulstone Hundred; Poplar Union]
(transferred to London, 1889) (created from Stepney, 1719)
OR C 1538-1905, M 1539-1896, B 1538-1862 (LMA)
BT 1629 (GL); 1798-1871 (no M 1841-71, no B 1855-57, 1859-61, 1863-71) (LMA)
Cop M 1629 (Ts I GL, LMA, SG, CRW); C 1770-1837, M 1754-1837 (LMA)

STRATFORD LE BOW **Baptist Chapel**, Old Ford f 1785
OR B 1814-37 (PRO: RG 4/4163)

SUNBURY **St Mary** (1,863) [Spelthorne Hundred; Staines Union] (transferred to Surrey
1965)
OR C 1565-1944, M 1566-1933, Banns 1907-15, 1936-58, B 1566-1654, 1661-1950
(LMA: DRO 7)
BT 1630, 1639 (GL); 1800-47, 1849-56 (LMA)
Cop M 1566-1812 (Ptd, Phillimore 4, 1912); M 1630, 1639, 1813-37 (Ts I GL, LMA,
SG, CRW); M 1813-37 (WMI); M 1566-1812 (Boyd); M 1790-1837 (Pallot Index);
C 1565-1875, M 1565-1876 (IGI)
Cop (Mf) C 1784-1875 (SG)

SUNBURY **Methodist Chapel** f by 1790, reb West Staines Road 1866
OR no registers known

SUNBURY **Independent Chapel**, Green Street f 1792, b 1817, reb 1900, closed 1968
OR no registers known

TEDDINGTON **St Mary**, Ferry Road (a new parish church dedicated to
St Alban the Martyr was b 1889, the old church kept as a chapel) (895) [Spelthorne
Hundred; Kingston Union] (chapelry in Staines, separate parish in 13th century)
OR C 1558-1927, M 1558-1921, Banns 1773-1810, B 1558-1680, 1695-1909
(LMA: DRO 125)
BT 1639 (GL); 1800-Apr 1809, May 1810-35 (no M 1833) (LMA)
Cop M 1560-1837 (Ptd, Phillimore 3, 1911); CB 1558-1812 (Ms GL); M 1639 (Ts I GL,
LMA, SG, CRW); M 1560-1837 (Boyd); M 1800-37 (Pallot Index); C 1558-75,
1584-1608, 1615-1840, B 1558-75, 1583-96, 1617-40, 1645-80, 1695-1861 (Ts SG)

TEDDINGTON **Chapel** (Nondenominational)
OR C 1810-11 (LMA: acc.1040)

THAVIES INN (175 in 1841; none given in 1831) (extra-parochial place) (Inn of Court)

TOTTENHAM All Hallows, Church Lane (6,937) [Edmonton Hundred; Edmonton Union]
OR C 1558-1896, M 1558-1899, B 1558-1901 (LMA: DRO 15)
BT 1629-30, 1639 (GL); 1800-12, 1814-68 (no M 1841-68, no B 1858-60, 1865-68) (LMA)
Cop M 1558-1837 (Ptd, Phillimore 9, 1938); M 1629-30, 1639 (Ts I GL, LMA, SG, CRW); C 1558-1625, B 1558-1620 (LMA); C 1813-28 (I only SG)

TOTTENHAM Meeting House, High Road (Society of Friends) (registers listed more fully in introduction)
OR Z 1727-1837, M 1662-91, 1727-1836, B 1667-91, 1726-1837 (PRO: RG 6/506, 543, 549-50, 840, 848, 1177, 1297)
BT B 1865-86 (LMA)
Cop Z 1727-1837, M 1662-91, 1727-1836, B 1667-91, 1726-1837 (Friends' House)

TOTTENHAM St Francis de Sales, High Road (Roman Catholic) f 1793 (Cath Dir 1965)
OR C 1794+, M 1795+ (gap 1823-27) (Inc)
Cop C 1794-1840, M 1796-1849 (Catholic FHS)

TOTTENHAM Wesleyan Chapel, High Road (Wesleyan Methodist) f 1817
OR ZC 1821-37, B 1819-37 (PRO: RG 4/378, 1339)
Cop ZC 1821-37, B 1819-37 (Ptd Mf, CRW and NMFHS, 1985)
Cop (Mf) ZC 1821-37, B 1819-37 (SLC)

TOTTENHAM Baptist Chapel, High Road f 1827
OR no registers known

TOWER of LONDON (433) (extra-parochial place) [Ossulstone Hundred; Whitechapel Union] (transferred to London, 1889) *see* **ST PETER AT VINCULA**

TOWER WITHOUT PRECINCT, OLD (280) (extra-parochial place) [Ossulstone Hundred; Whitechapel Union] (transferred to London, 1889)

TWICKENHAM St Mary, Church Street (4,571) [Isleworth Hundred; Brentford Union]
OR C 1538-1679, 1682+, M 1538-68, 1570+, B 1538+ (Inc)
BT 1629-30, 1639 (GL); 1800-Mar 1811, 1813-39, 1845-46 (LMA)
Cop M 1538-1812 (Ptd, Phillimore 1911); C 1538-1831, B 1538-1838 (Ts SG); M 1629-30, 1639, 1813-37 (Ts I GL, LMA, SG, CRW); CMB 1538-70 (BL); M 1538-1812 (Boyd); M 1800-37 (Pallot Index); M 1813-37 (WMI)

TWICKENHAM Methodist Chapel, Back Lane later Holly Road f 1800, reb in Queens Road 1880
OR no registers known

TWICKENHAM Independent Chapel, First Cross Road f 1802, reb 1844
OR no registers known

TWYFORD, WEST Blessed Virgin Mary, Brentmead Gardens (sometimes called Twyford Abbey) (43) [Ossulstone Hundred; Brentford Union] (chapelry in Willesden)
OR C 1722-50, 1766-79, 1793, 1809-1955, M 1730, 1831, 1848-97, 1911-66, B 1729-66, 1780-1893, 1910-42, 1954-88 (LMA: DRO 98)
BT 1810-34 (no M 1810-30, 1832-34, no B 1811-12, 1834) (LMA)
Cop M 1810-35 (Pallot Index); M 1813-37 (WMI)

TYBURN *see* **ST MARYLEBONE**

UXBRIDGE St Margaret, Windsor Street (3,043) [Elthorne Hundred; Uxbridge Union]
(chapelry in Hillingdon until 1827)
OR C 1538-1960, M 1538-1694, 1841-1942, Banns 1842-1952, B 1538-1924
(LMA: DRO 10)
BT 1629, 1639 (GL); CB 1800-03, 1813-15, 1817, 1819-35, 1840-43, 1847-70
(no C 1833-35, no M 1800-03, no B 1803) (LMA)
Cop M 1538-1694 (Ptd, Phillimore 5, 1914); M 1629, 1639 (Ts I GL, LMA, SG, CRW);
C 1757-77 (LMA); M 1538-1694 (Boyd)

UXBRIDGE Chapel, High Street (Independent and Presbyterian) f 1717
OR ZC 1790-1807, 1833-36 (PRO: RG 4/2332)
Cop ZC 1790-1807, 1833-36 (Ptd Mf, CRW and NMFHS, 1985)
Cop (Mf) ZC 1790-1807, 1833-36 (SLC)

UXBRIDGE Providence Chapel, The Lynch (Independent) f 1771 closed 1962
OR ZC 1789-1806, 1812-37, B 1812-37, 1847-55 (PRO: RG 4/1133, 1949, 1964, 2462,
2830); C 1854-1954 (Uxbridge Library)
Cop ZC 1789-1806, 1812-37, B 1812-37 (Ptd Mf, CRW and NMFHS, 1985);
C 1854-1954 (Ts I SG)
Cop (Mf) ZC 1789-1806, 1812-37, B 1812-37, 1847-55 (SLC)

WAPPING St John, Green Bank (3,564) (created from Stepney, 1729)
[Ossulstone Hundred; Stepney Union]
OR C 1617-1940, M 1620-1940, B 1620-1881 (LMA)
BT Mar 1803-Mar 1804, Apr 1805-61 (no M 1838-61) (LMA)
Cop C 1617-65, MB 1620-65 (GL: Challen 38, LMA, SG)

WAPPING French Church *fl*. 1711
OR no registers known

WAPPING Baptist Chapel (first meeting in Wapping, then in James Street, Stepney, then
in Little Prescot Street, Goodmans Fields) f 1633
OR Z 1786-1803 (PRO: RG 4/4283)

WESTMINSTER St Peter (Westminster Abbey), Old Palace Yard (185)
OR C 1607+, M 1655+, B 1606+ (Westminster Abbey Muniment Room)
BT CB 1813-37, 1839-55 (no C 1813, 1820, 1828, 1830, 1832-43, 1846, B 1853-55)
(LMA)
Cop C 1607-1875, M 1655-1875, B 1606-1875 (Ptd, HS 10, 1876);
B 1705-45 (Ptd, *Notes and Queries* 169, 1935)

WESTMINSTER The Most Precious Blood (Westminster Cathedral), Ashley Place
(Roman Catholic) b 1903; the Cathedral holds records dating back to the time of
peripatetic priests; several of these have been printed
OR CMB 1729+ (Inc)
Cop (Mf) Extr C 1729-1827, M 1729-54 (SG)

WHITCHURCH *see* **STANMORE, LITTLE**

WHITECHAPEL St Mary Matfellon, Whitechapel Road (30,733) (created a parish in the
early 17th century from Stepney) [Ossulstone Hundred; Whitechapel Union]
OR CM 1558-1940, B 1558-1857 (LMA)
BT 1800-21, 1825-39 (no M 1838-39) (LMA)
Cop M 1606-25 (Ptd, *New York Genealogical and Biographical Record* 19-24, 1888-93 (no
copy at SG but in Boyd)); C 1823-31 (Ts GL); C 1558-70, 1792-1831, M 1558-76,
B 1558-76 (Ts I SG); C 1711-39, 1766-1837, M 1713-1837 (Ts I only, SG)

WHITECHAPEL Baptist Chapel, Mill Yard, Goodmans Fields f 1600
OR B 1732-1837 (PRO: RG 4/4505-06)

WHITECHAPEL Presbyterian Church, Somerset Street, Goodmans Fields
OR C 1756-80, 1783-1811, B 1749-1826 (PRO: RG 4/4353, 4511-12)

WHITECHAPEL Baptist Chapel, Little Prescot Street, Goodmans Fields (previously
    meeting in Wapping, then in James Street, Stepney) f 1633
OR Z 1786-1803 (PRO: RG 4/4283)

WHITECHAPEL Beulah Chapel (Baptist) f 1653 (*see* **ST GEORGE IN THE EAST**)

WHITECHAPEL St George, Little Alie Street, Goodman's Fields (German Lutheran)
OR C 1763-1857, B 1763-1853 (PRO: RG 4/4570-71, 4543-44, 4572-73, 4603)

WHITEHALL PALACE, VERGE OF THE (238 with St James Palace)

WILLESDEN Kensal Green Cemetery, Harrow Road
OR B 1833+ (Cemetery)
BT B 1833-72 (LMA)

WILLESDEN St Mary, Neasden Lane, Church End (1,876) [Ossulstone Hundred;
    Hendon Union]
OR C 1569-1979, M 1574-1974, B 1572-1966 (LMA: DRO 113)
BT 1813-14, 1816, 1847-54, 1864-68 (no M 1814, 1853-68) (LMA)
Cop 1569-1865 (Ms Cricklewood Lib and Archives, 152 Olive Road, NW2 6UY);
    C 1569-1614, M 1569-1838, B 1572-1614 (SG); M 1574-1775, 1801-38 (Boyd);
    M 1800-37 (Pallot Index)